# DREAM
# TOOLBOX

# DREAM TOOLBOX

Building an Entrepreneurial Mind
and Financial Abundance

## KENNETH C. ALDRICH

DREAM TOOLBOX PRESS
LOS ANGELES, CALIFORNIA

*Dream Toolbox: Building an Entrepreneurial Mind and Financial Abundance*

© 2019 by Kenneth C. Aldrich

For information contact:
ken@kennethaldrich.com
www.DreamToolbox.com

ISBN: 978-1-7338242-0-0 (paperback)
ISBN: 978-1-7338242-1-7 (ebook: mobi)
ISBN: 978-1-7338242-2-4 (ebook: epub)

Library of Congress Control Number:  2019937854

Printed in the United States of America

Book design by Dotti Albertine

# CONTENTS

# ACKNOWLEDGMENTS

IN MY CAREER, I have written thousands of pages of contracts, business proposals, investor presentations and a wide variety of other documents. None of that prepared me for how difficult it would be to try to tell in a couple hundred pages, more or less, why I believe the development of an entrepreneurial mindset can change the lives of at risk young people and many adults who simply feel "stuck" in a financial stalemate. Whether this book changes lives or not, only time will tell, but it could not have been written without the following people:

Yvonne Craig-Aldrich, my wife and companion of over 40 years, whose example and memory inspired me to try to say something meaningful and who supported my volunteer efforts with young people, even while she was in the final stages of a two-year losing battle with cancer. Her wonderful book of memories from a life in ballet, film and television (*From Ballet to the Batcave and Beyond, by Yvonne Craig*) showed me how life experiences could be converted into a book that people would want to read.

Nadia Khalil Bedwan, who appeared in my life, as if by magic, several years after Yvonne's death, to become my love and companion, and whose experience in writing three remarkable books, even while raising two children as a single mother and caring for an extremely ill spouse, is a constant reminder to me that even when the world says, "you can't," the reality is that "you can." She writes of Love, Truth, Purity and the human soul, and has changed thousands of lives. See www.nadiakhalil.com.

Nancy Gale and kids of her "Ambition" classrooms (https://www.ambition.org), who have given me a real life laboratory in which to see if what I was saying had actual meaning to young people.

Alison Diaz, founder and CEO of Environmental Charter Schools (https://ecsonline.org), where Nancy Gale's students meet and where real life experiences make learning relevant for inner city students.

Anna Ouroumian, Refounder, President & CEO of the Academy of Business Leadership (http://www.goabl.org) has inspired me greatly. She has had a remarkable journey of overcoming tremendous odds. Her one-of-a-kind work with kids and innovative programs on mindset shifting, entrepreneurship, and wealth creation for over 20 years have changed the lives of thousands of diverse students. She has provided a forum in which I could interact with her scholars, and positively impact, and empower hundreds of her "kids" of all economic backgrounds to pursue their dreams and change their life trajectory.

Pamela Saunders, a superb specialist in SEO and all things Internet, without whose tireless efforts, the original DreamToolbox.com and all the blogs that now live there would never have been possible. Not only did she guide its creation, she made sure that many thousands of people found the site and its content. That effort was the beginning of this book.

Lori Miller, my editor, who took my random musings on the entrepreneurial mind and helped turn them into a coherent story.

Dotti Albertine, who did the heavy lifting to create a lovely cover, format the text, register in all the required places, and make this into an actual book.

# INTRODUCTION

LET ME TALK a bit about the structure of this book and what it is intended to be.

First, there is a massive amount of material available online and elsewhere that can help anyone who is trying to start and grow a business, which is what entrepreneurship is all about. However, what is not generally available is material that examines *what it means to think and act like an entrepreneur:* how to internalize a set of deep-seated beliefs about one's self and one's personal capacity that can change everything.

*Dream Toolbox* began as an online blog, and is not intended as a "how to" book, but as a guide to developing the mental tools that anyone can use to create financial abundance and freedom from worry. Part One outlines the mental tools you'll need to have in place to prepare yourself for a lifetime of success. In Part Two, you'll find some basic guidance on the fundamentals of starting a business. Once you get started, you'll find many useful books that go into more detail. I'll list a few as I go along here, and there are many more being written all the time. These you can find with just some basic online research once you've got your first start-up going strong.

Although originally conceived as a book for high school age students, I have realized that the tools and belief systems described here can be developed and used at almost any age. Looking at my own career, for example, I realize that, although I wish I had developed the belief systems and tools that made me successful earlier in life, I didn't really understand what I was doing until well into my 30's and had no real financial freedom until much later. That time was not totally wasted, but it was not efficiently used. I just didn't know the things or have the tools that I now want to share.

Therefore, the content of this book is intended for both the young and for older readers looking for a fresh start. *It is for anyone seeking financial freedom.* However, if you are an adult and find this material useful, by all means use it to make your own life better, but then, please pass it on to the young people in your life. They are our future.

## MY STORY

Before getting into any specific *tools* from the Dream Toolbox and how someone with an Entrepreneurial Mind can use them, you deserve to know who I am. Who is this guy who is purporting to provide ideas that might change your life?

For many years, I have been a successful serial entrepreneur and investor, which simply means that I've started a series of businesses, and most of them have been successful. I have also helped to finance a lot of other entrepreneurs trying to make their dreams come true. Some of those businesses have been spectacular successes, and some have been failures, so I have gotten to see the things that work and the things that don't. By the way, only the projects were failures, not the entrepreneurs. Many of those went on to great success.

My business experiences have changed my life, but it took me many years and a lot of luck to figure out the things I want to share with you. My goal now is to pay my good luck forward by saving those who study this book many years of struggle.

I did not inherit wealth. My first job was at age 14 as a carhop in a root beer stand at $0.25/hour. Later, I washed dishes, mowed lawns and worked minimum wage jobs from grade school through my college years before I was able to start getting higher paying jobs. My parents, who were by no means wealthy, helped me as much as they could, but more money was needed than they could provide, and I was often up before dawn to finish a job before classes began.

Once I finished college and decided I needed more education, I went out on my own to pay for law school and quickly got a taste of true poverty. Roaches, rats and assorted other "critters" and I became well acquainted in some of the places I lived, and protective steel bars on windows and doors became part of my existence. I vividly remember one particularly low rent apartment in which I had to chase roaches off my toothbrush each morning. I didn't enjoy that life, but I survived it and learned from it, and finally completed my formal education with a law degree from a quality law school.

Armed with that, I then got what should have been a wonderful job as a lawyer in a prestigious firm, but I quickly discovered that not all was a bed of roses. First of all, I realized that—at least in those days—young lawyers were similar to indentured servants serving out an apprenticeship. I knew my pay was pretty low, but I was shocked to discover that my secretary was earning more than I was. That was my first experience in what a friend of mine calls 'the going wage' or the minimum that an employer can pay without having the employee go to a different job. For young lawyers in those days, there really was nowhere else to go without losing the potential pot of gold that we all thought would come when we became senior associates and later a partner. So we stayed and hoped for raises and promotions.

By itself, that might have been acceptable. Senior partners did earn nice fees and lived in nice houses and drove nice cars, so there was something to look forward to. The real shock was realizing that, for me, there was no joy in doing what I was doing. I was working to help fulfill other people's (i.e. clients') dreams for their future, but working to fulfill other people's dreams was really not that much fun. I vividly remember a TV promo from that period for a show called *Wide World of Sports*. It showed a skier making a mistake and flying off the course to crash into a snow bank. The tag line was "The thrill of victory; the agony of defeat." I realized that, for me, practicing business law, my specialty, offered little or no prospect for the thrill of victory.

The minimum expectation for us as lawyers was that we would create foolproof contracts that would make everyone happy. But for me, there was no "thrill of victory" in that. It was just expected. However, there was ample opportunity for the "agony of defeat" if anything went wrong that I had not anticipated and prepared for. As far as I was concerned it was a case of "Heads you win; tails I lose." I stayed in that job long enough to be confident that I could practice law successfully and be a competent lawyer, but even though I was succeeding and getting promotions, the feeling persisted that I wanted something more. After a few years, I resigned and went to work as an investment banker.

This was more fun. I got to help put deals together and raise capital, so there were definitely moments of victory, but it still was not very satisfying. If successful, our clients had a very real victory in completing the purchase of another company or raising a lot of money from investors. My firm got a fee, but we were always the 'hired help'-- well paid, but never in control of our own destiny.

Then I got a lesson that was the first real step toward my becoming an entrepreneur. The firm I worked for lost a lot of money in its New York home office. Our branch in LA was profitable, but the firm was no longer solvent so it was sold in a "shotgun marriage" to another New

York firm 3,000 miles away. I might have gone to New York, but I had had enough cold winters to last a lifetime. I needed another job.

I quickly found one with a former client that was much more rewarding. This time, our firm owned its own "deals" and sometimes I earned bonuses from our successes. However, a few years later, the industry we were in experienced a major downturn; my company was sold to avoid financial collapse. Once again, I was again out of a job.

Finally, the light bulb went on in my head and I realized two things:

1. No job working for someone else was ever really more secure than my last paycheck.
2. The thing that kept the failure of my two employers from destroying me financially was that I had developed skills that I could market to lots of different kinds of companies.

I knew then that I had to find a way to be my own boss and control my own destiny. I wanted to be able to keep the profits I generated instead of working for others and hoping for a bonus that was not within my control.

I turned down multiple job offers and ended up out of work for 11 months before I finally figured out how to start my own first business. This experience changed my life. I have now been my own boss for over 40 years and have been successful enough that, for many years now, I haven't had to work on anything that did not give me pleasure and fulfillment. Yet, I work every day because there is nothing more rewarding and just plain "fun" than doing what I do—creating successful businesses.

I should note that I am not even close to being among the super-wealthy like Bill Gates or Warren Buffet, but I am comfortably within the "top 10%" that we hear so much about. For quite a while I thought I had just been lucky. As I began to do some research for this book I was surprised to discover how very much within reach the top 10% and sometimes even the top 1% really are. They are attainable for almost anyone who builds in himself or herself an entrepreneurial mindset and uses the tools that make up the Dream Toolbox. Being near the top of the economic ladder is to be part of a relatively exclusive club, but one that is unique for a very special reason: *anyone can join* if they make the right choices in selecting their dreams and pursuing those dreams.

I should also say that I am not a member of any disadvantaged minority. Some might say that I then have no basis to say that anyone can use these tools to achieve success. But it's important to stress that this is just not true. Because I had to start at the bottom, and had a lot of friends who were also starting there, I got to observe the struggles, failures and achievements that were the realities of life for many of my friends who also had the additional burden of belonging to one or more minority categories. There is no question that my friends suffered discrimination I didn't experience; yet they often achieved successes that were far greater than mine. They had to master some tools that I didn't need (or didn't think I needed) early on, and some of these tools propelled them to great successes years ahead of my own. I just wish I had learned to use those tools earlier.

I believe with all my heart that it is not race or gender, or even family wealth that divides the successful from the unsuccessful, but getting an education and realizing that each of us has the power, *now* and at every stage of our lives, to make the next stage better or worse.

The genesis of this book came from years of acting as a mentor and coach, mostly to at-risk high school students, but also to young entrepreneurs trying to find the path to success through a new business. One of the surprising things I learned was that, very often, a single illuminating event occurred that quite suddenly opened windows of unrealized opportunity to someone who had previously thought they had no future except poverty or life in a dead end job—or, worse yet, crime, prison or death on the streets.

Those moments of new light were often not the result of long hours in the classroom, but of hearing a single comment or example that was like opening a window in someone's mind so that they suddenly saw a whole new world of possibilities. This single moment of recognition did not create success, but it did open the eyes to what was possible. Once that happened, nothing was ever the same and hope replaced despair. A friend of mine calls these moments of insight *sparks* because they can light an inner fire that lights a lifetime of success.

That insight about *sparks* led to the creation of a series of 3-4 minute audio blogs aimed at at-risk young people in the hope that at least some who listened would experience their own spark of recognition and realize that there is a better life out there than anyone had ever told them they might achieve. Those blogs can be heard or read at *www.Dream-Toolbox.com*. They were the inspiration for this book

Those blogs and this book are not meant to be yet another "How to get rich" manual that almost no one can hope to follow. Instead, the blogs and the chapters in this book are intended to be aspirational explorations into the world of what is possible, so that the dreams we all have no longer seem beyond reach, but are attainable goals at the end of a journey of personal discovery.

This book is one small next step in my effort to make life better for as many people as I can reach. In it, I will be expanding the ideas from DreamToolbox.com, adding some exercises, examples, and some personal stories that I hope will make both defining the dreams that really matter to each of us easier, and achieving those dreams, seem possible.

Also, although most of the examples and stories I am including here relate to the creation of new businesses in the classic entrepreneurial sense, most of the attributes of what I call the *Entrepreneurial Mind* can be used equally well in the context of a job working for someone else. It just requires looking at the opportunity from a different perspective. I'll give examples of that when I can, but please use your own imagination. Not everyone has the desire to start some new business, but I firmly believe that every successful person does have a desire to be the best that they can be and to make whatever business or career they are in the best it can be.

However, to be financially free, every one of us needs to create an economic structure for our lives so that whatever job we may have, whether working for ourselves or someone else, becomes a tool to create economic freedom and independence. A job, no matter how good, does not equal financial success. It is a tool to achieve financial freedom, but only a tool and nothing more. We'll have a lot to discuss about that later.

So, how can you make the same thing—or more—happen for you?

**IT ALL BEGINS WITH WHAT YOU DREAM
AND WHAT YOU BELIEVE.**

# PART I

# DEFINING the DREAM and CREATING the ENTREPRENEURIAL MIND

# Chapter 1

# The Four Pillars

WELCOME TO *Dream Toolbox: Building an Entrepreneurial Mind and Financial Abundance.* The stories, exercises and history that follow here come from my firm belief that personal freedom is absolutely essential to achieving a quality life and that no one has true personal freedom unless they also have a level of financial freedom that assures a life free from financial worries.

All of us have the right to an abundant financial future, and building that abundant future is possible for almost anyone if they are willing to change four things in the way that they think about their financial life. The foundational pillars of financial abundance are really quite basic:

1. **Have a dream** that is both big and worthy.
2. Change core beliefs from *I can't* to *I can.*
3. Begin **today,** not in some distant future.
4. Build an *entrepreneurial mind.*

These things are especially important when working with young people. What they need from us as adults is not financial support, but emotional support and guidance to help them create a belief system that makes everything seem possible—because it is.

Every one of us is a possibility waiting to be recognized and realized. A friend of mine wisely says, "Never say, *It is possible*; instead say *I am possible*." The phrasing is a bit alien to the ear, but the concept is profound because it says that each of us has within us all the possibilities that life that can offer.

Let's examine these four pillars of change a bit more closely.

1.  **If you don't have a dream, how can you have a dream come true?** Enough said.
2.  **"Whether you think you can or you think you can't, you are right."** —Henry Ford. Changing core belief systems from *I can't* to *Yes, I can* is a change that anyone, including children at a very young age, can make, but it takes focus, dedication and, in the case of children, the loving belief of a parent or mentor.
3.  **Success begins now.** To make that kind of change in core belief systems, a person has to believe at the most fundamental level of their being that they have the power to take control of their life and fulfill their dreams of success and abundance, and that the power is not in some distant future, but is available today. We have to banish forever what I call the *Myth of Someday*.
4.  **Build an *Entrepreneurial Mind*.** An entrepreneurial mind is one that sees every obstacle as an opportunity. To develop that mindset involves changing, through daily mental exercises, the way we view the world and the risks and opportunities in it. It does not mean every person reading this has to become an entrepreneur and start a new business. It does mean that to achieve financial security and abundance, you need to learn to think in a

way that is quite different from the way most of us have been taught and the way our children are probably being taught in school even today.

Let me give you an example of the shift between traditional teachings about financial security and how the *Entrepreneurial Mind* sees it. One of the great myths that most of us have been taught is that having a great job is the key to financial security and wealth. This is simply not true. No one whose financial security is dependent on a paycheck is ever truly financially free. They are always one paycheck away from a crisis.

True financial freedom requires something more and different: a set of tools, including beliefs, mental habits, attitudes, and a way of looking at life and business that insures that almost any financial setback can be overcome. Having these belief systems and other tools are essential for creating an *Entrepreneurial Mind*, and no one who develops this mindset ever needs to fear losing a job ever again. Developing these tools is what **Dream Toolbox** is all about.

Changing dreams and belief systems from *I can't* to *I can* may also have a profound and beneficial effect on society at large. People who believe that they have the power within themselves to build and secure their economic future are far less vulnerable to demagogues who prey on fear and poverty to undermine individual freedoms.

# CHAPTER 2

# It Starts with a Dream

TOOLS ARE OF no value if you do not have a clue about what they should be used for. To put it in the context of an old saying, "If you don't have a dream, how can you have a dream come true?"

Most of us never really think clearly about what our dream for a better life would look like if it actually came true. Most of us just have a fuzzy wish to be successful, or perhaps famous. But that is not a useful dream. It is simply too hard to plan or strive for something this vague. As I will discuss at more length later, hoping for success is not a plan. Something more is needed. Instead, let me describe an exercise that can help anyone define their dreams in a way that makes those dreams achievable.

If you already have a specific set of dreams for your life, you might be able to skip this exercise, but I recommend that you do it anyway. You may discover a dream that is even bigger and more appealing than the dreams you already have. One of the saddest things I know is to see someone settle for a dream that is smaller than they really want and less than they could achieve.

The exercise is not a one-and-done event. I have used it many times and continue to repeat it anytime I sense that I may be losing my personal focus. In fact, long after I was financially secure, I found myself repeating this exercise at various times, just to help me define what new or emerging goals were really important to me. Perhaps doing the exercise will seem strange and your mind will want to say, *I must be crazy to think I could do that*, but I promise you that this exercise has real power. Here it is.

## Exercise: DREAM BIG

Begin with a blank piece of paper. Then give yourself 15 minutes to write down a list of all of the things you would really like to do *if you knew you could not fail.* Do it quickly and don't edit the list in your mind as you go. Your subconscious will try to tell you, *Don't list that; it is impossible.* List it anyway. The purpose of the exercise is to break the habit of listening to all the negative self-talk that our brains always engage in, the kind that says, *You couldn't possibly do that; you are too poor, or you will be discriminated against, or that is just impossible…* etc. Most important, do not edit the list as you write. Just put down everything that comes into your mind, no matter how wild, foolish or impossible it seems.

Once you have the list, then read it through carefully and put it away overnight. Again, don't edit anything yet. Let what you have thought marinate in your unconscious for 24 hours or so. Then take out your list and look at it with fresh eyes. Only then should you begin editing.

One warning when you begin to edit. Yes, it is OK perhaps to weed out some ideas that are really impossible, like flying without wings. But be careful about making assumptions that are too limiting. Where would we be if Wilbur and Orville Wright had said, *Man can't fly; let's take that off our list?*

Finally, look through your list for those things you truly would love to do but never dared to try because they seemed beyond any hope of success, and for those things you were too afraid of failure to try. Then pick one goal from the list, one about which you can say, "I really want to do that." Then, adopt that dream and start using the tools of the Dream Toolbox to make it real. Most importantly, **do the drill. Don't just think about it. Do it! You are likely to be very surprised.**

One final note. Once you have picked your dream, write it out in as much detail as you can. What would your life be like if the dream were already realized? Be as specific as you can. Without clearly defining your dream, how are you going to know when you have reached it? And be really specific. Otherwise, how will you know you are not settling for something less than truly fulfilling that dream? It is really easy to adjust our dreams downward to "be more practical," but that is usually just a way of quitting on the installment plan. Defining your dream specifically and writing it down—and even telling a trusted friend, if you have one who will support you and not bring you down with their skepticism—can be a powerful tool.

# CHAPTER 3

# Make It Real

THERE IS A second critical step in the process of making a dream come true that I personally used to reach my first 'retirement day,' the first day I really knew I would never have to work again. That was over a quarter of a century ago, yet I have never actually retired because I am having too much fun. However, I will always be grateful to the person who first taught me the tool I want to describe. It is a simple exercise that can bring your dream in from the future and make it part of the present. It is a mental tool designed to make your dream so much a part of who you are that your subconscious mind will find ways to fulfill the dream even when you can't see how it is possible.

The tool is a process I call *Active Dreaming*. (Others have called it *visualization*, and it has been known for many, many years under these and other names. What I can tell you from first-hand experience is that it works.) Here is what I did and what I recommend.

## Exercise: ACTIVE DREAMING

1.  **Recollect the dream**. In my case, I reminded myself of a specific Big Dream I had created and defined as precisely as I could, so that I would know when I had reached it. (Use the one you selected from the previous exercise, if appropriate.)

2. **Fill in the details. Be specific.** Once I had the dream defined, I filled in all the details in my mind. My original dream wasn't particularly noble—I had been poor a long time and I just wanted to be able to write a check for a million dollars and not have it bounce. I wanted to have financial freedom. So, I imagined every detail of what it would feel like to have the capacity to write that check and what the other parts of my life would look like—what kind of house I would live in, what kind of car I would drive, what the smell of the leather in that car would be, what it would be like to take the woman I loved to dinner and never worry if I could pay the bill? I created a whole life story for myself.

3. **Bring the reality of your dream to life, living the dream in your mind as if it were already true.** The key to making the dream real is not just to imagine in as much detail as you can what it feels like to have that dream be a reality, but to bring that reality to life in your imagination as if it had already happened. In my case, I looked in the mirror every morning and imagined how people would react to me if I were rich enough to write that check, where and how I would live, and who would be in my life. I tried to reduce all of those things, in as much detail as possible, to very clear images in my mind.

4. **Repeat this visualization daily.** The last step in the process is to live the dream in your mind **every day until you achieve it**. In my case, I created a whole life story for my dream and every morning for 10 minutes, I would live that dream in my mind. I didn't allow myself to think about how I would achieve it. *I imagined it as already being real, right then, not in the future.*

The beauty of the mind is that it can create future things and make them real today. We've all had that experience in the dreams we have at night. Sometimes we wake up and think they actually happened. That is the kind of clarity in the mind that *Active Dreaming* should create. I guarantee you will feel pretty silly doing it, perhaps for a long time, but eventually you will begin to free your subconscious mind to make it a reality. An odd result for me was that I became so good at thinking of myself as already successful that when I reached the point that I could actually write that check, I didn't notice for quite a while that I had reached my dream. It was important to recognize its achievement, because I then had to create a new dream that stretched my capacity and fueled my imagination again.

Of course, practicing *Active Dreaming* by itself won't realize anyone's dream. I still needed to use all the other tools that I knew of to pursue my dream in daily life, and I worked very hard at it. Over time, however, I realized that what I had done by Active Dreaming was to program my subconscious mind to see opportunities that I might otherwise never have seen, each once of which got me closer to my goal.

I will tell you that I felt very foolish staring at myself in the mirror—and I certainly did not let anyone know what I was doing—but I was desperate for a change in my life so I did it anyway. When I realized that I had reached my original goal, I also realized that the path I had actually taken to get there was significantly different than what I had imagined when I started the drill. *Without actually knowing it, my subconscious mind had made course corrections along the way that made reaching my dream possible.* I have never after that day doubted the power of the *Active Dreaming* exercise.

Let me give you an insight into how my subconscious guided my conscious efforts in this process. My initial plan was try to use the skills I had developed in the real estate business, either to become a consultant to investors and be paid with a combination of cash and ownership in the projects I worked on, or to find a financial institution or group of investors who would provide me the money to invest for them.

Both goals were proving very difficult to achieve, so I was supplementing income by moonlighting as a lawyer for a small firm founded by a friend. I was getting nowhere. I desperately wanted to move to Malibu beach, but couldn't begin to afford the prices. They were a tiny fraction of what they would cost today, but the average house was still beyond my means, particularly since I had no predictable source of income. Then two things happened.

The first was that a friend of mine mentioned that he had stumbled across a woman who had a very old and very tiny house on a beach in Malibu and she needed to move out and into a retirement home. All of this was true. The house was only 550 square feet in size. I had no job and my savings were dwindling. However, I saw myself as the person I had been imagining, the man who could write a million dollar check, so I decided that I absolutely had to make an offer on the house. The owner accepted my offer and, because she wanted a monthly living income instead of a lump sum of cash that she would have to invest, she agreed to accept a small down payment and be my lender for the rest of the purchase price. The interest rate I offered was more than she could get at the bank, and all she had to do was cash my checks once a month. She accepted my offer and I had my beach house. It was old and it was tiny, but it was mine. By the way, I never missed a payment and the lovely lady who sold me the house was delighted with our arrangement.

The second thing that happened was that a lawyer friend of mine said that he had a client who needed investment advice to diversify her portfolio holdings from the family stock she had inherited into some real estate. Although he knew a lot about real estate, my friend thought it would be a conflict of interest for him to be both her lawyer and her investment advisor. Also, his client did not want to pay any fees or salary, but wanted to pay only if the investments made were profitable.

That was definitely not the kind of money management I had in mind. I had expected some financial institution would be so enamored of my skills that it would pay me a fee *and* share profits with me, as was common for large money managers at that time. Also, I had just bought a house and had no reliable income. However, something in my subconscious said, *Do it*. I agreed to take no fee until there was a profit and the client agreed that once the original investment had been repaid, I could share in profits at a higher rate than was customary where fees were paid in advance. In short, I agreed to risk working for a long time for no money in exchange for a chance to make a lot without having to invest any money of my own. That was good for me because I had no money of my own to invest at the time.

The safe thing to do would have been to turn down both opportunities, but I firmly believe the reason I didn't was because, in my mind, I already knew I was successful and that the money that would demonstrate that success was bound to be available as needed.

On the other hand, our arrangement was not just a foolish gamble. I knew I was buying the house at well below what it would be worth once it was cleaned up and made market ready. I also knew that, because of my preparation and experience in the real estate market, I was very likely to find investment properties that would meet my new client's criteria.

Those two decisions led to my fulfilling my first Big Dream of being able to write a million dollar check and to live on the beach in Malibu. (The Malibu part had been part of the lifestyle vision I had created in my *Active Dreaming* exercises.) As I predicted, Malibu real estate was poised to go up in value and I was able to buy and sell several more houses until I had enough money to start buying apartment buildings. I was also right about my ability to buy profitable real estate for my client, which led to my finding other people who needed the same services but did not have access to large-scale real estate hedge funds.

As it turned out, I actually didn't write a million dollar check until some years later because I found I could build on prior successes to raise all the capital I needed. I eventually did write one against my own bank account, but not until it represented only a small share of my assets. Still, the clarity of my goal and the certainty that I had the power and skills within me to take the calculated risks that led to that check-writing and home ownership success all started with the reprogramming of my subconscious mind to believe I had that power long before I had the physical assets to back up my belief. This is the power of *Active Dreaming*.

# CHAPTER 4

# Believing in the Dream

NOW I NEED to introduce an important distinction. Having a dream and visualizing it is only part of the solution. Each of us also needs to create a belief system about our own power that is unshakeable.

Henry Ford, the man who created the beginning of the automobile industry we know today, once said:

**WHETHER YOU THINK YOU CAN,**
**OR YOU THINK YOU CAN'T, YOU'RE RIGHT.**

I am convinced that there is no more important concept to understand than this if we want financial success. Our *belief systems* determine where we will end up in life. I am not talking about religious faith, although that can be a huge help if it is strong. I am talking about those fundamental things we believe about ourselves.

Without a change in fundamental beliefs from *I can't to I can*, success is very unlikely. The core beliefs about what we can and cannot do are embedded in us by parents, family and friends almost from birth. Yet sometimes, well-meaning family can be the worst, undermining even our best efforts at defining a dream and visualizing the fulfillment of that dream.

Let me give you a personal example to illustrate this. I spoke at a conference for high school and middle school students a couple of years ago, telling my own story of coming from a family in which no one had ever finished college, to attending Harvard University. During the question-and-answer period, a young woman who was considering where to go to college told a similar story. She had the grades and SAT scores to get into the college of her dreams, but everyone around her, including her family, friends, and even school counselors, had told her, "Don't do it. You won't fit in with all those rich kids. They will look down on you and you won't succeed."

At this point in her telling her story, I interrupted to say, "That is nonsense. Don't believe it. I entered Harvard as a poor kid from the Midwest who was terrified of the rich prep school kids who were in my class. Within weeks, none of it mattered because we were all in the same boat, struggling to learn the same new and exciting things. You can create your own success." She burst into tears and said, "No one has ever told me that I really could do it. Thank you." I later learned that she had been accepted at a prestigious college. I have no doubt she will end up near the top of her class.

What changed? In that moment, her *belief system* about what was possible for her had shifted.

Let me give you another personal example of the power of our beliefs and how they become the tools of success. Quite a few years ago, I was approached by a man I knew only through a mutual friend. He had little formal education, but had a real estate license, a small real estate company, and the dream of building a high-rise office building using a construction technique that had never been tried in an earthquake area like LA. What he did not have was any experience or track record of having done such a thing. And he had no money. Neither did I, at the time.

We had a third partner who had grown up in the construction industry and knew a lot about construction, but he had never built such a building on his own. What all of us had, however, was the absolute belief that we could do it. With that team and that dream, we set about to build our building.

Almost all our friends thought we were crazy, and I thought so too, at times. I vividly remember going from investor meeting to investor meeting, dragging along a model of our dream building that could barely be carried by one man (this was before 3D graphics were available). And I remember leaning out the open door of a helicopter hovering at the height where the 30th story of our building would be, to show a prospective investor the view that a premier tenant would have when the project was completed.

I also remember the day I read in the paper that our first investor, supposedly one of the richest men in the world, the man who had promised to fund the entire project, was pulling all of his money out of the US. He would fund nothing for us. We had to start the hunt for a new investor all over again and persuade our banks not to foreclose on the property.

However, a few years later, a 30-story high-rise office building lined the skyline of an LA suburb, a building that had withstood a major earthquake that validated our faith in the construction methods we had fought for. I can also tell you that in the several years that it took to put that project together, we had many other 'near death' experiences in our business. But what made it all work was that we looked at each of these crises as simply problems to be solved, not proof that we were doomed to failure. In short, we believed in our dream.

How did that happen? We had some luck, of course, but everyone has luck many times in life, both good and bad. The difference was that each of us in his own way had developed a core belief system that said,

Yes, I can. We had good luck along the way, and bad, but that core belief system allowed us take advantage of the good luck and find ways to deal with the bad. Based on our lack of prior experience, we had no right to succeed. But we thought we could, and so we did. As Henry Ford said:

**WHETHER YOU THINK YOU CAN,
OR YOU THINK YOU CAN'T, YOU'RE RIGHT.**

# CHAPTER 5

# Changing Belief Systems

IT IS WELL and good to talk about changing our belief systems from *I can't* to *I can*. But how do you actually do that? In recent years, I have thought a lot about how we can change our belief systems to redefine what we believe is possible. The *Active Dreaming* tool I have just described is a powerful first step. The rest of the transformation will come from diligently using the tools we will talk about in subsequent chapters, but there is a significant additional element that is critical for each of us to add right away if we truly want to replace failure with success in our expectations of what is possible and what is likely.

That additional element of success is replacing negative self-talk with perspectives of reality that help us build a better belief system. What does this mean?

When presented with a challenge that takes them out of their comfort zone or blocks hoped-for possibilities, most people immediately begin playing a tape in their heads that lists all the reasons why they should not take the action needed to meet the challenge. It feels like a downturn or a failure, even. But, as we all know but frequently ignore, challenges to the status quo almost always present us with an opportunity, as well. What makes the difference between success and failure is our beliefs about who we are and what is possible. The first step is to redefine challenges as opportunities.

I still remember a friend of mine in high school who had a terrible time getting dates with the girls he admired. I was no great Romeo, but I usually did not agonize much about getting a date for the events where a date was important. I had a rather normal adolescent social life. One day, I asked my friend who was having so much trouble, how he went about asking for a date. I discovered that his usual approach was to approach a potential date, usually a girl he had admired or longed for but had been too shy to get to know socially, and say something like, "You wouldn't like to go to the movies with me, would you?" No wonder he seldom got a date.

But much more important was what his approach said about his core beliefs about what was possible. He just didn't believe the outcome—a girl who wanted to go out with him simply saying, "Yes, I'd love to"—was possible. He was running a negative tape of rejection in his head, long before he ever asked for an actual date.

Unfortunately, most of us have similar negative tapes in our heads about other things. *I just can't do math. I could never give up my job to start a company; that would just be too scary. What if I should take on that project and it failed? What would people say then?* The list goes on and on, and each of us has played some of these tapes in our heads at one time or another.

People often spend many thousands of dollars and thousands of hours in psychotherapy exploring childhood experiences to understand why those have led to current neuroses. But that is not what I am exploring here. I am talking about relatively normal people like you and me who learned in childhood or sometimes at a later age that success could not be expected, and so we adopted a default response to see challenges not as opportunities but as instances of *I can't* rather than *I can*.

We will explore specific systems to change core belief systems in more detail later, but the important thing at the beginning is *simply to realize that a negative tape is beginning to run,* and to learn to ask some self-reflexive questions like, "Is that really true?" Often the answer is, "Not really" or "I don't know." Either it is not true or we don't know it to be true, so there is no reason to assume something bad when something good might be equally likely, or perhaps more so. The question itself stops the knee-jerk negative self-talk, and that's the beginning of the looked-for change.

I recently got a call from a friend whose business history had been filled with successes. But he had recently had major financial reversals, partly because of medical issues that kept him from working as hard or long as he was accustomed to working and had put him in the hospital several times. However, at long last, the pain was under control with new medication.

His question to me was, "What do I do when the pain comes back?" I asked him if the doctor had said that it would. He said, "No, the doctor had told him that if that happened they would deal with it." Still, his doubts persisted, "But, what will I do then?" With this negative loop running in his head, I knew he had no chance of success. When last I heard from him, he was still bogged down in his self-manufactured negative thoughts.

When it is someone else, like my friend, it is easy to see how playing a negative tape even enabled him to ignore his current good health. Instead, he saw only the possibility of failure, not the promise of success. How different his life would be if, whenever he found himself worrying, he simply said, "My doctors have said that whatever happens in my medical life, we can deal with it. Meanwhile, I am free to make a success out of my business again!" The hardest part that each of us needs to master is to hear the negative tapes when they begin to run in our brain and simply turn them off by asking the questions, "Is that really true?" or "How do I know that is true?"

In my own case, I have learned that each time a negative thought pops into my mind, it is more likely than not grounded in fear instead of in reality. Of course, if the fear is legitimate, if, for example, I am about to do something physically dangerous, then I have to take that fear seriously and evaluate the risk. But most of the time, the fear is really one of looking foolish to friends, or fearing that I will be a failure as a person if the project I am about to undertake should fail. Once I identify the source of the fear, I can usually turn it into something positive. We'll discuss more about the fear of failure later, but, for now, my suggestion is just to become aware of the negative message that your brain is sending and meet it with an affirmation of the belief that *Yes, I can*. Let me give you another example.

Relatively early in my career, I made the decision to leave a secure job as a lawyer in a big and powerful firm to go into a much riskier profession for which I had no formal training, and in which my success or failure would be determined by my ability to close financing transactions. When I disclosed my plan to some of the lawyers I worked with, I discovered an interesting thing. Even though I was taking a pay cut and assuming a much greater degree of risk, some of my colleagues were openly jealous of my change. Others loved their legal work, were happy with their career choices and simply wished me well. But it was the hostility and skepticism of the doubters and the jealous that surprised me, and it certainly added fuel to the doubts I already had. What I didn't understand until much later was why. If what they wanted, and were jealous of me for having, was a change of career, why not just make the change for themselves instead of envying me?

Of course, once I had time to think about it and had some experience in what making such a change involved, I knew the answer. They were afraid of looking bad in the eyes of their colleagues, afraid they would fail and have to come back with their tails between their legs begging for their old job back, and perhaps afraid they would not get their jobs back—or another as good—and thus disappoint their wives or children. The latter two concerns are real, but simply require the courage to say, *I can do this.* The first reason, embarrassment, is so absurd that it would be comical if it weren't so tragic. I will be forever grateful that I didn't let fear of ridicule ruin my dream.

In reflecting back on those days, I believe the critical element that allowed me to move forward was that I looked honestly at the risk I was taking. I realized that I could survive even the worst that could happen if I took the chance, and knew that I didn't want to continue down what seemed to me to be a road to nowhere I wanted to be.

Henry David Thoreau wrote many years ago, "The mass of men lead lives of quiet desperation." I think it was the desperation of knowing they lacked the courage to change their lives and were thus doomed to live below their best selves that drove my colleagues to envy. If they had honestly looked at the risks of making a change versus the certainty of continuing the life they were living, they would not have experienced the desperation and the envy that I saw.

By the way, this story is not intended to demean the many wonderful friends I have who love the law and are brilliant lawyers as a result. But those who love it have chosen to do what they love, not because they wrongly believed they had no other choice, but because it's what they really wanted to do. Instead, the story is intended to reinforce the absolute necessity of changing our core *belief systems* so that the default response to any challenge is *Yes, I can.* We'll get into some of the specific tools for making that change in later chapters.

# Chapter 6

# The Myth of *Someday*

THERE IS A myth that pervades the way most of us were brought up, which is that success will somehow come (if it ever does) in some future *someday* because of a fortunate promotion, or by being discovered, or by gradually working our way up some ladder of success.

Any of these things could happen, but what makes this way of thinking so destructive is that it ignores one of the most powerful tools we all have—the power of the mind. I know of no formal study that has ever been made, but my own experience with successful entrepreneurs, and what I have read about others whom I have never met, convinces me that in almost every case, those people believed at the core of their being—long before they actually became rich or famous— that they already had the keys to wealth and success within them and did not need anyone else to give them constant *Attaboys*.

There is an oft repeated saying, "Fake it until you make it." But behind that glib phrase is a powerful truth. If you can wake up every morning already knowing in your very bones that success is inside you, the subconscious mind takes over and seeks out ways to make that happen. We have talked about this already, but it is worth repeating—often.

This doesn't change the fact that most successful people have spent thousands of hours developing their skills before they achieved what the world often thinks is instant success. But what most people miss is that just spending those thousands of hours is meaningless without the core belief, *I am already a success*, and the equally important definition of clear and definable goals. You could say, *I am destined for success* to yourself, but that is not as powerful because it puts success in the future. The real success is the day you begin to see yourself as successful **now**, with the cars and houses and other badges of success to come later.

I told you earlier the story of my own visualizing of my success. But all the while I was waking up each day and seeing my dream as a reality, I was still doing all the things I needed to do to build my first business, working long hours, adding to my education, and planning ahead. I still had to put in the thousands of hours needed to achieve the financial rewards I wanted, but once I made that image of being already successful a part of my mental DNA, those hours no longer seemed like work. Instead, they were just part of the course I had to run to get a finish line that I already had reached in my mind.

Let me suggest a very valuable exercise that can help anyone seeking to develop a mindset of success. First, make a list of things you want to have or to achieve in the future; then rewrite them this way: "I am _____ " describing in as much detail as possible what life will look and feel like when these goals are achieved, and writing it in the present tense. For example, "I am (not I will be) the founder of a successful medical device company that will improve the vision of hundreds of thousands of people."

I really lived that dream of being a founder of that optical company. I was actually a co-founder because I had a partner who was as tenacious and committed as I was, which is a huge advantage in any start-up, as we will later discuss. The company that he and I started was ultimately sold for several hundred millions of dollars and the technology is now part of medical procedures that improve the vision of thousands of people every year.

What I want to stress, however, is that it never occurred to us that we had to wait for some future event before we could begin. We had no capital of our own to fund the company and our initial concept required that we overcome an entrenched and powerful company selling what we thought was an inferior product. But we trusted our research and launched the company anyway. We could have waited to try to find some academic researcher to authenticate our concept by giving it his or her stamp of approval, but, as is the case with all new companies, there is a time when you just have to begin. Saying, "This is going to be tough; I think I'll wait until I have more money saved, or some scientific paper is published that validates our idea," or whatever excuse we might have found for delay would have resulted in our never getting started at all.

I mentioned earlier my experience when I decided to leave the safety of law practice and go into the world of business. Many of my colleagues were astonished that I did not wait for some corporation to hire me into a high paying and secure job. But that would have meant putting my dreams on hold, waiting for some external person or event to provide success for me. I could have waited my whole life waiting for that *someday* to occur. Yes, there was a risk in starting a new career on my own timetable. There almost always is. Years later, some of the people who envied me for following my dream, but who had decided to wait for the right time, *someday*, were still waiting.

The reality is that *someday* almost never comes, because those who put off starting the pursuit of their dreams will never find that risk-free *someday*. We all know some of those people. That doesn't mean that we should take foolish risks just for the sake of change. It does mean that if we want to pursue our dreams, there is a time for action, and waiting for the perfect *someday* is just an excuse for never taking a risk and never achieving a dream.

There is a particularly pernicious form of the *myth of someday* that effects, and infects, many young people. We are conditioned from the day we first enter the school system that we need to wait for permission for everything, whether answering a question or going to the bathroom. By the time we get to high school or college, the belief has become so ingrained in us that before we can tackle any major project, we need approval and support from some senior person.

This is a recipe for perpetual mediocrity! If Mark Zuckerberg had waited for some professor at Harvard to tell him he had a good idea and should drop out of school to pursue it, we would have no Facebook today. The same is true for Bill Gates, founder of Microsoft, who changed the world of computer software and became one of richest men in the world.

Could these people have failed in their efforts? Absolutely. But they also could have started over, gone back to school later and lost only some time. Had they not pursued their dreams, chances are good they would not have pursued any other dream, living instead what Thoreau called "lives of quiet desperation." There is always some risk in following your own path, but at least for me, the alternative is a life of stagnation and frustration.

By the way, this does not mean that everyone has to drop out of school or quit their jobs. Opportunities often exist within companies, and higher education can be a great launching pad for many satisfying and successful careers. The point is that it's okay to break the mold of always needing permission to live our dreams. We need only learn how to take calculated risks and have some courage.

**SOMEDAY HAS A WAY OF NEVER COMING AT ALL UNLESS IT IS CREATED NOW.**

# CHAPTER 7

# The Entrepreneurial Mind

WE HAVE NOW talked about the first three steps in making dreams come true: clearly defining the dream, changing core belief systems, and beginning now instead of waiting for some future *someday*. The final step, particularly if your dream has anything to do with financial success, is to develop what I call the *Entrepreneurial Mind*.

There is a very famous statement made by the writer F. Scott Fitzgerald that goes like this: "Let me tell you about the very rich. They are different from you and me."

Fitzgerald was both right and wrong. The rich are very different from most people, but not because they have more money. Instead, if they have made their own wealth and not just inherited it, they will have developed a way of looking at life that is simply different from how most people in the world look at life. And that makes all the difference.

I call it the *Entrepreneurial Mind*, and it is an enormously powerful tool. It is the difference between those who rise to the top 10%--or even the top 1%--of the economy, and those who wonder why they haven't. It is also something that anyone can learn and develop if they really want to.

The best way I can illustrate the process of change from conventional thinking to the *Entrepreneurial Mind* is a very personal example.

As a young man, I used to have a fantasy that one morning I would wake up rich and never have to work again. I did the things I have discussed in prior chapters until they became part of my routine and I didn't really think about them except as part of my daily life. Then, one New Year's morning as I read the morning newspaper, I realized something: I didn't have to work that year—or any other year, ever! Nor would I have to lower my standard of living or change my lifestyle.

An even greater realization came later—and that is what I want to share. I didn't get to financial and personal freedom because I started out rich, or was smarter, or won the lottery or a Las Vegas jackpot.

What really happened was that, over time, using some of the techniques we have already discussed, I was lucky enough to realize that the power to change my life was within me and not dependent on anyone else's rules. My mind had learned to see every challenge as an opportunity, not as a dead-end alley.

My wife used to be amused—and sometimes annoyed—that I instinctively always had at least three alternative plans to achieve whatever I was trying to do, just in case the first or the second didn't work out. But it was the belief system underneath that habit that was really important. I had reached the point at which I simply could not believe there was not some way to solve whatever problem I faced. Except for death and taxes, I have never seen a problem in life that I didn't believe could be solved.

Sometimes, the personal or economic cost of solving the problem at hand is more than the solution is worth, so the sensible thing is to move on to something more rewarding and a better use of the time we have. This is why most entrepreneurs learn to embrace failure as part of the learning process, and put their failures behind them quickly once they realize that the cost of salvaging the project is not worth the loss of what might replace it. But the belief that every problem has a solution is incredibly powerful. It means we get to choose which problems to solve and which to put aside in the quest for something even better.

Building this kind of mindset takes time and constant attention. It also requires that we take responsibility for everything in our lives, never assuming that what happens to us defines us. Things will happen to each of us, both good and bad, but what defines us is our willingness to take 100% responsibility for how we react to both the good and the bad. The entrepreneurial mind instinctively looks for opportunity. The failure mind looks for someone or something else to blame or looks at good fortune as somehow undeserved. This deprives the recipient of the good fortune of the joy of achieving and replaces it with the fear that the good fortune will be snatched away.

In talking recently to a good friend who is quite successful, we realized that neither of us feared losing the wealth we had accumulated because we trusted completely that we could rebuild if we needed to. Neither of us plans to have to do that, but knowing that our success was not just chance and that we had developed the tools to make it happen again as needed gives a great sense of freedom. That may be the reason that so many people who achieve sudden success as film or TV actors are still frightened by life. They aren't sure they could ever do it again. Those who have carefully built an entrepreneurial mindset and learned to use the tools we talk about here, in *Dream Toolbox*, need never have that fear.

Your definition of success can be anything from wanting to create highly successful companies to wanting to cure cancer, but if you can't wake up every morning wanting to achieve that goal and loving even the tedious things you have to do to get there while using all the tools in your toolbox, then just get a job, put in your 40 hours per week, enjoy the day-to-day pleasures of living and hope that the pension they promised you will actually be there. For some, this is enough. For me, it would have been like a slow death.

Most of us are programmed from a very early age to believe that a lot of things are just impossible for us, that we are too poor, too uneducated, from the wrong ethnic group or have the wrong skin color to succeed. These negative belief systems can destroy our dreams.

I could tell you story after story, all true, about friends of mine who have started with nothing but a belief in themselves and achieved incredible successes. One was an orphan in a war-torn foreign country who came to this country with no money and without speaking English, yet went on to reform and run a significant non-profit organization that has helped teach thousands of kids the power of changing their belief systems and how to be entrepreneurs even at ages as young as 12.

Another friend was once a young man who had to flee from Iran after the revolution, at the risk of being put to death by the revolutionaries, arriving in New York with little more than the clothes on his back. Prior to that, he had been beaten and tortured during the civil war in Lebanon because he was wealthy and some of the rebels wanted his property. By the time he arrived in New York, he had made and lost two fortunes through war and revolution, and he was back at ground zero with a badly damaged body and no money. Today, he is again a highly successful businessman in Los Angeles who gives 25% of his personal efforts each week, and many dollars each year to worthy charities.

Another friend is a woman whose mother was murdered, she herself was raped, and her business was destroyed. She is now an up-and-coming businesswoman who has founded a charity to teach entrepreneurial skills to young people. Each of these people is now happy and successful. The reason is that they each believed that they had the power to create their own successes, no matter what had happened to them from the outside. And they did just that.

How can this be done? You replace every negative thought that tells you why you can't succeed with one that says, *Why not? I can do that.* It takes time and practice, of course, and there are many resources -- books, courses, and mentors that can help you get there. Perhaps the key to it all is to believe and act as if you were *already* the success you intend to be, and to make that the overwhelming priority in your life.

A very powerful tool for building an entrepreneurial mindset is to make a list of the many times that both good and bad things have happened to you. List as many things as you can think of. Then review the list, asking, "What could I have done to *own* that situation, so that what I made of it and how I used it was within my control, even if the situation itself was not."

With practice, it will become second nature to ask that same question in real time whenever there seems to be a roadblock on your path to success; it will even help when you're facing a potential disaster for your company or your plans.

The same principals are true in business and in your personal financial life. I have made decisions, as every successful investor or businessperson I know has made decisions that were simply wrong, decisions that resulted in real losses, or even in the failure of a business. Mistakes are inevitable. But it is what we do next that matters most.

# CHAPTER 8

# Problem Solving

PERHAPS THE MOST striking difference between those who have an entrepreneurial mindset and those who don't is how they approach the problems—whether in business or personal life—that everyone faces.

The conventional thinker immediately looks to see if there are known solutions on the Internet, in books, among friends, and so forth. If none are found, he or she concludes they can't proceed any further, and gives up, looking to do something else.

The person with an entrepreneurial mind instinctively sees every problem as a possible opportunity. Rahm Emanuel, former chief of staff to President Obama, is famous for saying, "Never waste a crisis." He was talking about politics, but the same is often true in life and business.

In business, the fact that something is not working and someone, or a lot of people, need it to work, perhaps desperately, means that whoever can solve the problem has the potential to create a new product or a new business. And the lovely truth is that there is probably no problem that can't be solved, except perhaps death itself, and some people I know are working on that.

Long before I was born, every document was written by hand. Then Guttenberg invented the printing press with movable type and, quite literally, changed the world by making written knowledge available to almost everyone.

When I was a kid, if you wanted copies of a document, you put in multiple sheets of carbon paper, and heaven help you if you made a mistake. You had to correct it on each and every copy. Then Xerox developed the copier and once you had a perfect original, you could make as many copies as you wanted.

Then others created the computer-driven word processor, and then making a typing mistake was trivial. The computer even corrects your mistakes for you (often with the wrong word, but that's another story).

If I may get personal for a moment, let me tell you a true story. When I was in high school, I needed to take the SATs to get into a good college. I had studied Latin for four years because that was essentially the only language course my high school offered. (Either I was a very bad student or the teacher wasn't very good, or both, but when I got to college, I found I couldn't even translate the Latin inscription over the gates.)

But before that, I had to take the SATs, one section of which was languages, which in my case was Latin. The test consisted of a long passage from Caesar's *Gallic Wars*, and I couldn't read it—a phrase here and there, perhaps, but I simply couldn't get past, "Omnia Gallia in tres partes divisa est." I could have just quit, but fortunately, even then, I had a mind that was wired to look for solutions.

So I read the questions, which were in English, and discovered that if I used the few phrases I could translate, I could eliminate some obviously wrong answers. Then I realized that some of the questions depended on answers covered in earlier questions. From this, I could begin to tell what the story was about and that gave me the answers to even more questions—without ever knowing the Latin at all.

I handed in the test, convinced I had failed in spite of my clever attempt, only to find out later that, not only had I passed (they never told you your actual scores in those days), but my score was so high that

I was exempt from further language requirements at a very prestigious Ivy League college—and I still couldn't read the inscription over the college gate.

I tell that story, not because I am proud of my genius. Anyone with a willingness to look for alternative solutions could have done the same. And I certainly don't tell it because it says anything good about the SAT testing of those days. I tell it because it illustrates the difference between the mindset that automatically assumes that if the answer can't be found in the ordinary way it does not exist, and the mindset that says, "There has to be a way to do this; how can I find it?"

I was lucky that I seem to have been born with that instinct. And it is one that absolutely can be learned by anyone willing to do the hard work of changing his or her mindset from one that sees obstacles, to one that sees only puzzles to be solved and opportunities for success.

One very practical first step whenever a problem arises that looks impossible to solve is to develop the mindset that says, ***There is always a solution.*** When faced with a problem, take a step back and say, *This is not a barrier; it is only a puzzle that I can solve because I know there is a solution. I just have to find it.* This is an incredibly powerful mindset to have.

I recall once, fairly early in my career, when I had managed to convince my bank that the real estate projects I was developing had great promise and merited a large unsecured line of credit. They loaned me almost a million dollars on my signature and I was a happy camper. That changed suddenly when there was a financial crisis in the banking industry. The bank suddenly demanded that I repay them in full in 30 days. What I owed was many times my net worth at the time and the real estate was nowhere near ready to be sold. This didn't look like an opportunity or a problem that could be solved to me; it looked like a huge brick wall that was about to fall on my head.

Then a friend said something rather wise. He said, "If you owe the bank $50,000 and you can't pay them, then you have a problem. But if you owe them $1 million, then they have a problem." This gave me a whole new range of possible solutions. I went to my bankers, explained the reality of their situation and mine, and worked out a way that they got paid and I got to complete a project that today repays me its entire cost every year. But it all started by my looking at my situation through a different lens of thought.

The lesson of all this is pretty simple. A problem is only a problem if you fail to see it as the opportunity it really is. If you think of problems as puzzles to be solved and not as barriers to success, the solutions will usually come.

## Exercise: PROBLEM SOLVING

As with many of the things discussed in this book, there is a very useful exercise that can help enormously in developing the muscle that is your brain into a problem-solving machine.

1. Write down the three most pressing problems you face.
2. Think about and then write down at least three different ways you might be able to turn each problem listed into an opportunity for change or growth of some kind.

This may be hard at first, but with practice, this exercise can produce results that are sometimes amazing. I have found that just writing down problem-solving ideas, even if they seem ridiculous, can sometimes be very helpful. In ways that I don't really understand, writing things down seems to tap into unconscious reservoirs of thought that may result in a completely out-of-the-box solution.

The most valuable by-product of this exercise for me has been that, after doing it for a while, the process itself becomes automatic and I find myself solving problems in my sleep, during exercise sessions, or just driving in my car. I firmly believe that the brain is like a muscle in the sense that the more you push it beyond its comfort zone, the stronger it gets. The bonus is that you can't sprain your brain by over-use, so it is a lot safer that what we are all tempted to do in the gym.

# CHAPTER 9

# Goals and Way-points

WE HAVE INTRODUCED the four pillars of dream building. Now it is time to get a little deeper into the details behind some of these concepts. First of all, there is profound truth in the saying we talked about earlier: **"If you don't have a dream, how can you have a dream come true?"**

But something needs to be added to this. Fulfilling a dream usually involves meeting a series of goals along the way. If you don't develop some measurable, intermediate goals that tell you if you are moving toward or away from your dream, how are you going to achieve it? Dreams worth having are seldom achieved in a single leap. Instead, the interim goals that need to be achieved along the way are the building blocks of dreams fulfilled. To do that job, the step-by-step intermediate goals need to be very clear and measurable. These interim goals are the stepping-stones to realizing the dream, and, when you reach an intermediate goal, you also have the right to celebrate the accomplishment of something important.

Equally important, establishing clear goals that mark the successful completion of each step toward the fulfillment of the dream itself is the best way to measure your progress. Think about the first manned space flight to the moon. That was a big audacious goal, particularly when you recall that the US started that program before we had ever even flown in space and that the whole mission was accomplished using computers that were not as powerful as the smart phone in your pocket.

But the other remarkable thing about that achievement (and it is true of every successful entrepreneurial venture I know) is that most of the time, that moon rocket was off course. Minute course corrections and adjustments were constantly being made. But, those corrections would have been impossible without a very clear understanding of where that rocket needed to be at each step along its flight path. Unfortunately, the intermediate goals in our entrepreneurial dreams are not always that clear. But they need to be. Otherwise, you never know if you are off course or not.

For many years, I raced small sailboats, and loved it. It also offers a great example of the relationship between a dream and the course you need to chart to reach that dream. One thing that is true about sailing is that you seldom can go in a straight line to your destination. Instead, reaching your destination involves a series of what are called *tacks*, which essentially means that you sail in a certain direction until you reach what is called a *way-point*, then you sail in a different direction to the next way-point until you finally reach your goal. It is a zigzag course that is actually the quickest route to success in the wind conditions that prevail at that time. There were several lessons that I learned from sailing that have been very valuable to me in business.

1.  **The shortest route is not always the fastest.** It depends on the conditions around you. In sailing, these include the wind direction and speed; in business, the market conditions and competition.

2.  **Without planning ahead to determine the way-points at which a change in direction was needed, victory was simply not possible**. True, wind conditions and other factors might change in the course of a race, but without a plan, the competitors would have simply sailed past me to their own victories. That was no fun for me, so I

learned to plan better. Without defining these way-
points, I would never recognize when changing
conditions were taking me away from victory instead of
on my constantly changing course toward the finish line.

One of the drills that every entrepreneur should do—and few actually do—is to spend a ridiculous amount of time developing a very short
and simple description of what the purpose of the business he or she
is creating should be.

I'm not talking about those lofty and vague Mission Statements that
the textbooks on entrepreneurship often tell you to write. If you can't
describe in one or two sentences what your business is actually designed
to do, you probably haven't given it enough thought. A friend of mine
likes to say, "It has to be so simple a gorilla could understand it."

Think about the statement, "The Ultimate Driving Machine." No
one with any exposure to TV or radio advertising will fail to recognize
that as the tag line for a BMW auto product. But it is also one of the
finest descriptions of a business goal I have ever heard. A million things
have to come together actually to build that automobile, but asking,
"Will this help create the Ultimate Driving Machine?" can be the test
of every decision that is made. Is what we are about to do getting closer
or farther away from that goal? That kind of clarity has real power.

I'm not arguing that BMW has achieved their goal, but could anyone in that company possibly not know what the goal is? If you can
articulate what your business is designed to achieve that clearly—even
if it takes a few more words—you will be well on the way to achieving
that goal.

The opposite is also true. As I look back on 30 years or more of
reviewing the business plans of start-up companies in which I have

invested or contemplated investing, one of the most common themes of those that failed was the lack of a clear purpose for the company. Oh, they all had the purpose of making a lot of money, but those that succeeded had a more specific purpose. Whether it was to find a cure for cancer, provide a financial tool that young people could use to start their financial future, improve the outcomes from cataract surgery, or any of many other goals, those who succeeded had a clear and lofty goal that was so well articulated that no one in the organization could fail to understand it, and could use it as a guide to daily action.

Those that failed almost always had goals that were fuzzy and did not go very far beyond, "I want to make a lot of money." This is usually a roadmap to failure.

It all starts with clear goals, both in your long term dreams and in your interim way-points. Without them, you will never know if you have succeeded or failed.

What I have found very useful is to get all the key players in any venture together in a room, turn off the phones and electronic devices, and brainstorm every idea any of us has as to how to define the goals of the company. It is not easy. Even as I am writing this, I am involved in a company for which that is proving a very difficult task because each of the key people involved believes they understand the goal, but the task of articulating it in terms that will be properly understood by everyone involved is proving difficult. What we know for sure, however, is that we cannot effectively move forward without achieving that clarity, because until we can explain it in a few simple words to someone else, it is highly likely that we who are the founders are not yet clearly seeing the same goal. We will solve that puzzle, but it illustrates how difficult defining goals can be. I have had company executives spend all day and have to start over again the next. It is that important.

# CHAPTER 1

# Hope is Not a Plan

THE PROPER ROLE of *hope* in our dreams is one of the hardest concepts to get right. With every dream there is always the hope that it will succeed, but if we have done a proper job of visualizing our dreams and mapping the way-points that will fulfill the dream, then hoping for fulfillment of that dream without doing something more is essentially a step backward.

Hope, for most people, implies a wish that someone or some external force will intervene in our lives to fulfill that hope. Then hope becomes just another manifestation of the myth of *someday* that we have talked about. I learned this the hard way in my own career. For a long time, I knew that I was discontent with the practice of law and the life that it would mean for me. Yet, what I did was simply hope that a better alternative would present itself, that someone would offer me my dream job and all would be wonderful. It was a lot like a fairy tale in which I was hoping for a prince charming to save me.

Only after I realized that this was *never going to happen* and began to take steps to recognize and fulfill my own dreams did anything happen. I began to make discreet inquiries about openings in business situations that would enable me to get some experience beyond the technical practice of law. In those days, and perhaps still today, lawyers were not considered by most people to be particularly capable of running a business and I certainly knew that I would be lost if I were just thrown out into the world to start my own. I needed a training ground.

What I did was conduct a search for someone—anyone—who would hire me in a business and non-legal function where I could learn how to be a businessman. Fortunately, a man for whom I had worked as a lawyer decided to take a chance on me. The pay was a lot less than I had been making as a lawyer, and I had no guarantee that I would not be fired anytime my boss thought I was no longer likely to add profits to his business. Frankly, I was terrified.

Fortunately, I had already developed work habits of discipline and was willing to learn whatever I needed to know instead of assuming that because I had a law degree I knew everything. The truth is that I was terribly naïve, but learned quickly. The group with which I was assigned to work made a substantial profit in our first year and it was clear to my boss that I had contributed to that result. More important than my boss noticing that, however, was that I realized two things: 1) that I still had an enormous amount to learn, but 2) I had the capacity to learn what I needed and no longer feared to put my career on the line and trust my ability to adapt and survive.

From there I went on to another job that provided me additional skills, and finally decided I was ready to go out on my own, which I did. The rest is my history, which has become a pretty wonderful life. It started with finding a customer who would pay for what I had to offer and building on that.

So, what does any of my story have to do with hope? A lot, I think. Hope would not have moved me out of the safety net of my safe but unfulfilling job. Hope would have left me still wishing for some external event or person to save me from taking the risks that changed my life. I had to do more than hope. I had to make the changes on my own and take real career risks to achieve my dream.

In spite of my success, I realize that I was incredibly lucky because when I jumped out of the safe world I knew, I had not yet learned most of the things that I can now write about as part of this *Dream Toolbox* series of stories. My Big Dream was not yet clear in my mind. I had no idea what way-stations I might need to reach, and the concept of active dreaming was totally alien to me. I was a high-wire act without a net.

However, I did do one thing that made all the difference in spite of my woeful lack of knowledge. I shifted *hoping* for a better life from wishful thinking into positive action, and that made all the difference. Had I known then the things I know now, I would never have said to myself, "I hope I can find a more rewarding career and survive in it." Instead, I would have already seen myself as successful and would have already been living with total clarity in my mind the dream that I had chosen. For me it would have been just a reality that had not yet happened.

My recommendation to anyone reading this is simple. Leave *hope* for those things that would be nice, but over which you have no control (like perhaps hoping the home town baseball team goes to the World Series), but make your dreams a reality in your mind today and enjoy the process of watching those dreams come to fruition in the real world beyond your mind, always knowing that the reality you create in your mind today is the reality that the rest of the world will see tomorrow.

## Moving Beyond Hope

A first step in this process is determining and defining who needs and will use the services and products you hope to provide. In my case, what I had to do was determine what skills I had that I could market to a new employer and what skills I needed to learn to create a business of my own; then I needed to make a plan for obtaining these skills.

If you are past that point and are ready to launch a business, the same principles still apply. You need a *market*, which involves knowing who needs and will pay for your product, services or skills. The key is to get into your market but also to allow for the possibility that your initial assumptions may be wrong. In this case, you may need to have sufficient reserves of capital and time to make changes as necessary. Surveys are nice, but the only real test is to try to sell what you have to the market you think will buy it and see what happens. If possible, launch your efforts with a test campaign in a relatively small segment of your total market. In fact, a classic technique is to offer slightly different versions of pricing, advertising copy, or even variations on the product itself in different parts of your market, then see what works best. Even if that is not possible for some reason, maintaining flexibility is a critical skill.

Let me give you an example of how success can still occur, even when the initial assumptions prove to be wrong, if the focus remains on identifying who the real customer is and how to reach him or her. Quite few years ago, I was approached as a member of the Tech Coast Angels, a large Angel Investor group in Southern California, by a young and impressive entrepreneur. The need he had identified was quite specific and seemed like a viable basis for a new company.

What he wanted to do was solve the problem of young people who could not shop on the Internet because they were too young to get credit cards, and did not want or could not use their parents' credit cards. The idea was to provide a debit card that could be purchased in retail stores like Rite Aid (the first outlet) with cash from an allowance or personal earnings. The need was real, the target customers (teenagers) seemed pretty easy to identify and to reach through social media, and there were a lot of them. And, the company had a key contract that provided a retail distribution channel.

The company raised the initial capital it needed and launched the product. Because I was on the Board of Directors, I had a front row seat for what followed. As the Company quickly discovered, the market proved much harder to reach than we had thought and not nearly as many teenagers as we expected bought the cards. That could have been the end of the story and an investment loss. Instead, the CEO, one of the most creative entrepreneurs I have known, looked for other available markets.

What he discovered was that many of the initial buyers were not teenagers at all, but older people who, for whatever reason, did not have bank accounts or good enough credit to get credit cards. He then shifted the focus of the company to that market. That shift in marketing focus changed everything, but it was based on paying attention to who was actually using the product and adjusting accordingly. Many other changes have happened since then, but that little company that began with a few million dollars of investor capital is now a $3 billion company on the New York Stock Exchange.

Teenagers still use the product, but are a relatively small part of the customer base. What happened was that the company, by paying constant attention to its customers and their needs and wants, was able to identify a much larger market than the founder and his investors ever dreamed of. There is an old saying in retail, "Know your customer." Ultimately, it is all about identifying your customers and meeting their needs.

My friend always had hope for success of his venture, but he also realized that hope is definitely not a plan and that hard work and careful attention needed to be paid to who his real customers were and what needs they had that his company could fill. That company remains today one of the most customer-focused I have ever known, and that focus shows in its success every day.

# CHAPTER 11

# What Is a Job?

WE HAVE ALREADY talked about the fact that financial abundance and security will never come from a job. So what is the value of a job?

Everyone needs a source of current income to pay bills. A job can do that for as long as you aren't fired, the business closes, or you find you can't work for health or other reasons. Then, a job becomes useless, sometimes overnight. I have known of more than one company in which the employees went home after work one day, then came back the next to find the doors closed and their jobs and their incomes gone.

A job is not useless. In fact, it can be hugely valuable once we realize that it is a tool, just like all the other tools in the *Dream Toolbox*. But the minute we start thinking it is more than a tool, we begin a process of becoming a loser in life. So what are the best functions of a job?

1. **Use it to build assets**. The first way in which a job can be used as a tool is as simple as taking a portion of each paycheck and investing or saving it to use when an opportunity presents itself. For most of a decade before I went out on my own, I did that. I saved sometimes as much as 30% from every paycheck and invested it. I wasn't trying then to find the next Google; I just wanted to build a financial cushion so that I could work without

income for as long as possible when that became necessary or valuable. I wasn't making much money. When I started work as a young lawyer, my secretary made more money than I did. I think my income in those years went from $7,200/year in 1965 to $35,000/year in 1975, but by 1975, I had $100,000 in my investment account, most of it just savings from my job.

As it turned out, having savings made all the difference. With that *tool*, building *assets* with income from my job, I was able to go without work for almost a year, invest in my start-up real estate business and take a first giant step to becoming financially independent.

2.  **Use it as a learning tool**. In the critical years that I worked for other people, I realized later that I was learning every day the skills that I would need in order to be a successful entrepreneur later. How much more I could have learned had I made *learning new skills* a priority I will never know. I didn't yet understand the concept of making almost everything in life a tool for success. But I must have learned something, because by the end of those 10 years, I found I had the tools to start my own business, to persuade others to believe in me and provide me with capital, and to make that capital grow once I had it.

I couldn't have done this if I hadn't been paying attention to the things that worked and those that didn't in the businesses I was working in. In fact, two of those businesses became insolvent and had to be sold at fire sale prices. Strangely enough, even that gave me confidence, because I was able to say to myself, *I don't think I could possibly mess up an opportunity any worse than the companies I had worked for. Maybe I could actually do better and be successful.*

Beyond that confidence, which was perhaps tinged with a bit of arrogance, I had paid attention to the things that worked and those that didn't. For example, I learned (fortunately, not with my own money) how dangerous borrowing could be if one used short-term loans to finance investments that had a longer term expected holding period. One of the companies I was working for was making a lot of money borrowing from banks and in the commercial paper market at low rates, and then lending that money to development companies on longer-term loans. We made money because interest rates on the short-term loans made to us were lower than the rates we could charge on longer-term loans. We were making money on what is called the *spread* between our cost of money and what we could earn by lending it out. This worked like a charm—until it didn't. Something happened called an *inverted yield curve.* Suddenly, the cost of money we were borrowing in the short-term market was higher than we could earn making longer-term loans. We were losing money on every transaction. I never made that mistake in my own business.

However, although it has nothing directly to do with the value of a job as a tool, I should also let you in on a secret that I don't really like to admit. I only learned part of that lesson. Ten years later, I had persuaded my banks to lend me $800,000 based on my personal credit and a good track record of doing successful real estate deals. The money from the banks was on what was called a revolving credit account, meaning that every 30 days or so the interest rates might change, but (at least in those days) I didn't have to pay the bank loans off until I wanted to because I had a profit from one of my projects and was flush with cash.

That was also wonderful—until it wasn't. One of those crises that occur periodically in the banking industry happened and I got a notice from my bank that said, "You have 30 days to pay off your loan." What they didn't say was that if I did not, they would file a lawsuit to collect and effectively put me out of business. Somehow, I cobbled together a lot of small loans and investments from people I knew who had learned to trust my integrity and ability, and I was able to pay off the bank and move forward.

I learned several lessons from that experience.

- **Think about the lessons learned from one experience more broadly**. I should have realized that what I was doing with my bank was as dangerous as borrowing short and lending long had been for my former employer.

- It is almost impossible to overstate the value of **building a reputation for honesty and ability.** Without that, my business would not have survived.

- If the business one is fighting to save is worth saving and the business model is valid, then it is critical to save it from the inevitable crises that every business faces. I call these *near death experiences* and almost all successful businesses I have known have had to survive at least one of these crises before reaching success. In my case, the business I saved the day I paid off my bank now produces about one third of the income that I wake up each January 1st knowing I will have for the year, whether or not I do anything else.

- **Use your job to build credibility.** One of the great things about working in almost any job is that it provides at no expense to you the opportunity to *build a track record* of achievement, integrity, work ethic, and a lot of other intangibles that go into the formula for success. My business could not have survived the crisis I just described if I had not had a network of people I could call for help in a crisis. And they could not be just people that liked me. They had also to be people who had seen me perform in difficult circumstances and perform day in and day out, good days and bad. Ultimately, any entrepreneur needs to build that in the context of the businesses he or she creates, but the process, and the habit patterns and trust of oneself can begin as early as the first job as a floor sweeper or barista.

In summary, a job is just a tool, but it can be a powerful one, particularly when it's used as the diving board from which you leap into the bigger pool of creating new businesses that will create new jobs (tools) for others.

# CHAPTER 21

# Zero Sum Games

WE NEED NOW to talk a bit about one of the most important concepts you can ever learn about building wealth and financial freedom. It is actually quite simple and can be summed up in one phrase: *Success is not a zero sum game.*

What does this mean? Think about any sports contest. Whether it is baseball, football, or any other competition, there is only one winner. Second place is only the first loser. But financial success is not like that. Think about Apple Computer, the most valuable company in the world as I am writing this. One of the reasons that Apple is so successful is that it has created platforms on which independent developers can produce and distribute apps that can make their creators very wealthy very fast.

Every time one of those app developers creates a successful app, Apple computer gets richer. But here is the important distinction. Apple does not get rich by making the app producer poorer. It gets rich by making the app producer richer. This is the exact opposite of a zero sum game. It is a game in which success by one party increases the success and wealth of the other. This is how business in a free society works at its best.

Are there exceptions? Sure, in some rare cases there is competition in which there is only a winner and a loser. I own an interest in a company that frequently bids on US and foreign contracts. These can result in revenues of tens of millions of dollars, and in those bids, there is only one winner. But notice something even here. In order to increase our chances of success, we often form partnerships with companies that have people with skills our people lack. This increases our chances of winning the contract, but it also means we have to share the income from the contract if we win.

Is that bad? No, quite the opposite. By sharing the wealth and the skills of two companies, we increase our chances of winning more contracts. Thus, even where there is a clear winner and loser, the players who share skills and profits are more likely to be successful than those who do not.

Let me give you another personal example. Many years ago, I was part of a team that was helping an owner decide which of several bidders was going to acquire some real estate worth hundreds of millions of dollars. One investor was the clear favorite, but he made a crucial mistake. He tried to drive such a hard bargain that no one else could benefit. My clients heard his pitch and walked away from the negotiations. In business, you often hear the saying, "You have to leave something on the table for the other guy." This bidder did not understand that. He wanted it all. What he got was nothing, and another bidder, who offered some attractive benefits to the seller, my client, won the contract. He gave up something in the beginning, but ended up one of the richest men in the world as a result. He understood that life (and business) is not a zero sum game.

If you can apply this principal in life and business, always looking for ways to make those around you wealthier as well and looking for ways to make the result of your own efforts greater by cooperating instead of wanting everything for yourself, you have taken a giant first step toward success.

Success in business is not a Zero Sum Game. If you try to make it one, you are almost guaranteed to lose. Help others succeed and you will help yourself.

I had a partner once who was one of the most brilliant and creative people I have ever known when it came to finding opportunities that others simply never saw. But he had a problem. Some part of his brain always felt he was losing something if the other side made money. He saw business as a zero sum game. I, on the other hand, was relatively poor at seeing opportunities, but was good at finding ways that both parties in a negotiation could walk away feeling they had made a good deal. Together, we had a solid partnership, but one of the things that made it work was that my partner was willing, once the basic structure of the deal had been agreed upon, to step back and let me do the closing. We made a lot of money together as a result.

Before leaving this subject, please notice something important that may pass you by. I just admitted that I am not particularly good at spotting opportunities, something that I stress as an important entrepreneurial skill. I wish I were better, but I am not. What I do know, however, is that these skills are very important. Because I am an entrepreneur with an entrepreneurial mindset, I have adopted a simple, but highly effective, strategy. I look for and surround myself with people who have the skills that I lack and who need the skills I do have.

In the forecourt of the Temple of Apollo in ancient Greece there was inscribed this maxim from the Oracle of Delphi: *Know Yourself.* This means knowing where you are weak and where you are strong and using that knowledge to increase your chances of success. That is probably why most successful businesses have at least two founders. Almost none of us have all the tools we need for success. Knowing that and finding collaborators who make us better is a key to the entrepreneurial mind and entrepreneurial success.

# PART II

## THE NUTS AND BOLTS OF BEING A SUCCESSFUL ENTREPRENEUR

# CHAPTER 13

# Getting Started

WE HAVE TALKED a lot about changing core belief systems, visualizing your dream and making it real in your mind, as well as creating useful way-points to make sure you stay on track. These are all critical pieces in making any dream come true.

But now it is time to talk about more mundane things. The first of these is the importance of **just getting started**. For most people, dreams remain just that—dreams—and are never realized because of a critical missing piece. Unrealized dreams belong to those who simply never took the first practical steps to make them a reality. So let's talk about those first, critical steps.

1. The first is to **take a hard, realistic look at where you are in life and where you want to go**. If you have no money and perhaps belong to a minority, or are young, or have other significant obstacles that stand in your way, don't pretend they are not real. Instead, start thinking about what you will have to change about yourself, your surroundings, your education, or your lifestyle so that you might be able to turn these obstacles into stepping-stones to success.

   I know that I have said that those kinds of obstacles do not define you or prohibit you from achieving success.

*But,* and this is a big 'but,' if you don't address them realistically, they can block your success. I'll give you an example. I had a business partner a few years ago who was an incredibly talented black man. I noticed that when we went to business meetings, he was inevitably the best-dressed person in the room, and that when he traveled, he always carried a travel iron and pressed his clothes before each new day.

I asked him why, and his answer was simple and insightful. He said, "Although I am confident of my ability, I know that in any meeting I may encounter those who expect me, as a black man, to be less capable. Being always the best dressed person in the room helps to keep that issue off the table and requires very little effort on my part." I asked if he resented having always to be just a little bit better than his competitors. His answer was wise and accurate. He said, "Everyone has obstacles to overcome. Mine just happens to be skin color, but the things I do to make sure this is not a barrier to my success can also give me a better chance of success, even when my skin color would not have mattered in any particular meeting. So, by solving one problem, I have created extra opportunities. Why should I resent that?"

2. **Prepare to succeed**. Begin by doing the things we have already discussed and whatever else you have determined needs to be done for you to succeed. Above all, remember the words of John Wooden, perhaps the most successful basketball coach of all time, who said, "Failing to prepare is preparing to fail."

I once invested a small amount of money in a retail business. I would have invested much more, but as I worked with the founder to develop his business plan, I realized that, no matter how much I urged him to do so, he was incapable or unwilling to do the hard work necessary to prepare his financial projections for the months and years ahead. His attitude was, "I don't know what is going to happen; I can only do the best I can each day and hope for success." In spite of what I still think was an excellent business opportunity, he failed. The reason was simple. He failed to realize that *hope is not a plan*. By refusing to plan for the future, he was unprepared for the things that could go wrong and gave up when the first major barrier appeared in his way. Also, because he had not done basic planning, no one would invest the money that might have saved the business when it confronted its first major obstacle.

By contrast, another friend of mine started a new business some years ago. He had raised what seemed like a reasonable amount of money, but soon ran into cash shortages because, as the business grew, it required more cash than he or I had expected. However, he had done his homework and thought through the question, "If I need more capital, what do I have to create now so that I can attract additional investors?" He did what he had planned to do, was able to raise capital when he needed it, and now has a company that is highly profitable, with millions in annual sales.

3. Finally, **just start**. This sounds simple, but when any of us faces the uncertain future and looks closely at the risks that are involved in trying to make a dream that matters to us come true, it is very easy to say, "I'll start first thing

tomorrow." Procrastination is the greatest thief in the world; it steals our lives, one day at a time. Whatever your age or circumstance, you have the power *right now* to begin reshaping your life for success. **Just begin—now.**

We all know the steps that have to be taken. We need to do our market research, we need to determine what it is going to cost to run the business, we need to determine what the cost of each product is going to be or what the cost of delivering each unit of service will be, and we need to take a realistic look at how many units of sales it will take to get enough revenue to make the business profitable, how long that will take, and how much capital will be required to survive until that happens. These are all are just basic steps in building a business plan.

Once we acknowledge that these are just the building blocks of a business, it becomes a lot easier to simply take them one step at a time and move forward. Trying to imagine doing everything at once is daunting and sometimes paralyzing. Taking one step at a time, but understanding what the end goal is and what steps remain to be taken is critical. It sound easy, but it is not. However, breaking things into manageable pieces makes is possible

However, the final word is still the same.

## START.

# CHAPTER 14

# Thinking and Action

I RECENTLY READ a saying attributed to David Upton, a famous professor at the Harvard Business School. The statement was, "Don't avoid thinking by being busy."

There is a profound truth in this statement that many entrepreneurs (including me) often miss. We hear all the time that being an entrepreneur requires a willingness to put in 80-hour weeks, sleeping frequently in the office, and a variety of time-consuming activities. My own experiences over four decades of observing entrepreneurs and being one is that, in most cases, the 80 hour week is either a myth or represents an incredibly inefficient use of time.

Running as fast as you can is of no value, and is probably harmful, if you are running in the wrong direction. What is often far more important is taking the time to think about what needs to be done to reach the next goal on the path to success and how to reach that goal most efficiently. This requires time to think and a willingness to step back from the daily flurry of work and do that thinking. Thinking is often much harder than actively 'working', but is actually the most difficult, and most productive 'work' that an entrepreneur can do.

Let me give you a couple of examples from the world of sports, which is often a good place to look for both ideas and inspiration. Many years ago I was privileged to sail across a large chunk of the South Pacific with a man who had been navigator for one of the successful yachts in the infamous Fastnet 1979 boat race, in which over 300 yachts began the race and over 200 were either lost at sea or retired from the race due to severe storm conditions. Fifteen sailors were killed in the storm and many more had to be rescued after their boats sank.

What I learned from my friend and from written reports about the race was that the tactics that were most successful were either to sail a course that was a much longer, but ultimately much safer, path around the storm or to simply heave to, in which the boat is stopped in a position to ride out the storm safely, even though it may be blown far off course. The thing that did not work was continuing to race forward on the original course toward the finish line without thinking about how circumstances had changed. This required 'thinking,' not 'working,' and is a very useful reminder that very often in a new business (and sometimes in an older and profitable one) time out for thinking is required.

But thinking is not something anyone else can see and, to a third party looking in, can be indistinguishable from daydreaming or even sleeping. Our human nature rebels at seeming to do nothing, particularly when surrounded by our colleagues and employees who are working their tails off to keep the business going. But sometimes, doing nothing is the best course.

Let me give you another example from the world of sports. In soccer, there is a thing called a penalty kick, in which one player lines up approximately 35 feet (11 meters to be exact) from the goal and tries to kick the ball into the net while the opposing team's goalie tries to block that goal. During penalty kicks, the goalie will almost always try to anticipate where the ball will be kicked and dive at the last second toward that side of the end zone to block the shot.

However, about half the time, the goalie guesses wrong, and while he or she dives one way, the ball is kicked the other and the opposing team scores. In 2007, a study revealed that a better statistical result could be achieved by the goalie staying put in the center of the net.

Nonetheless, even today, goalies rarely behave that way. Why? I would guess, and some goalies have admitted, that they simply don't want to appear to their fans and teammates to be 'doing nothing.' Thus, they dive to the right or left and are destined to be wrong about two thirds of the time. Had they studied existing research, then engaged in some strategic thinking, and risked the disapproval of teammates and strangers, their success ratio could have been much higher. (See *WSJ*, July 7, 2018, for article describing this phenomenon.)

Sometimes, it is simply better to stop, think, and then act on those thoughts, than it is to continue doing what everyone else is doing, but trying to do it faster or longer. I have found this very true in my own career. I was married for many years to a wonderful woman who understood this—and me—very well. Every so often, when I was at my busiest, she would say to me, "Get out of here! You need a few days in the sun." I would protest that I was too busy, but she understood that being 'too busy' was exactly the problem. Then, she would ship me off for a few days to some tropical resort to lie in the sun and sip drinks with little umbrellas in them. Inevitably, I fretted for the first day or so, then relaxed and came back with new perspectives that changed my business for the better.

As I got better at the concept of sometimes thinking instead of hurried action, I often didn't need a week in the sun. I would simply take myself away from the office for an afternoon or a day to think through what was really important and what was not. What these sessions enabled me to do was to better separate the **important** from the **urgent**, and I gradually learned that the important and the urgent are seldom the same. The urgent is often defined by someone else's needs and desires rather than those things that are genuinely important for the success of the business.

**So please remember not to avoid thinking by just being busy.**

# CHAPTER 15

# Create Your Own World

ONE OF THE great joys of being an entrepreneur is that you get to create the life you want and shape it your way. I read recently somewhere a phrase that I liked a lot. "Don't plagiarize the lives of others; create your own." There is a subtle, but very important distinction hidden in that phrase. Earlier, we talked about the great value of learning from the experiences of others and not trying to invent everything yourself. That remains true if applied to specific skills that you need to develop, but just trying to copy someone else's success is a rather certain way to assure failure or mediocrity.

In the days of Apple's early success and the rise of online companies, it seemed to me that every start-up founder who came to me for funding was copying Steve Job's habit of dressing in black shirts and pants. It quickly became a negative indicator for me, because it said that the person I was interviewing probably was focused on superficial 'look alike' things and not on anything substantive. That was no doubt often a wrong assumption on my part, but it became a prejudice I had to discount to find the truth.

On the other hand, there were lots of things worth imitating and learning from in those days. For example, the graphic user interface was soon adopted by everyone in the industry, as was the touch screen when it came along. These were new ideas that made a real difference in our lives. There is a saying that, "Ideas are the currency of life." This is very true. One of the marks of someone who has mastered the tools that make up the entrepreneurial mind is their ability see in day-to-day events and activities some fresh applications for old ideas.

So, what do I mean by creating your own world? Most of the great entrepreneurial ideas became great by addressing what I call a *friction point* in life, sometimes an obvious one, but often not. For example, the creation of text messaging and, later, of apps like Twitter and Instagram filled the increasing need for rapid communication without the formality of an email or phone call; however, the fact that this was a *friction point* in communications was largely unrecognized until someone came up with these really new ways of communicating.

I work a lot in the world of biotech and medical devices. One of the more successful companies I founded became successful when we realized that surgeons who were replacing cataracts (which they had been doing for generations) were not able to give their patients clear vision after the surgery. Cataract surgery involves replacing the lens inside the eye that has become cloudy with a clear synthetic lens that can restore clear vision. However, because no way to measure the exact power needed in the newly implanted lens had been developed, the results were often poor vision even after the surgery.

We were trying to create a device that did the same thing as other devices did in LASIK surgery, but did it a bit better. But since there was no real *friction point* to be resolved, just an incremental improvement, no one was interested. Then, a physician with whom we were working pointed out that we could solve a major *friction point* in a different kind of surgery. Several years of work and some significant investment got us to the development of a final product. In the end, the company went from having a value of $5 million to a final sales price of over $300 million.

We were getting nowhere so long as we just tried to do what everyone else was doing a little bit better. We succeeded when circumstances showed us how to do something no one else had even thought of doing and then apply it to a different kind of surgery.

My partners and I did the same kind of thing when one of them (not I—that is the value of having good partners) realized that the wind energy business was beginning to grow in other parts of California and that desert land near Palm Springs was selling for very little because it was perceived to be almost worthless land where nothing would grow, and no one wanted to live because it was too hot and windy. However, the wind blew almost every day and was highly predictable, exactly what's needed for a wind energy farm. We built the first wind energy park in the area and today, wind turbines produce an enormous amount of energy from the area, land values have increased dramatically, and I get to cash checks each year that exceed my total investment in that project.

The point is that there is a fine but critically important, line between just copying what everyone else is doing, and seeing how a small alteration might change an industry. Don't copy. Build on what exists and create the new.

# CHAPTER 16

# Fear of Failure

BELIEVE IT OR not, one of the biggest obstacles to achieving financial freedom and an abundant and successful life can be summed up in three words: FEAR OF FAILURE.

Notice that I did not say failure. I said *fear* of failure. In reaching any goal worth having, there will be failures along the way—often many of them. It is the fear, not the reality, of failure that dooms most people to lives of frustration, lives far below their potential.

The reasons are actually quite simple. Fear of failure does several things, all of them bad.

1. It persuades us never to try.
2. It makes us give up on ourselves or our dreams at the first major barrier.
3. It paralyzes us at exactly the times when bold action is needed.
4. It undermines the inner belief of *I can.*

To deal with the fear of failure, we first have to look the possibility of failure itself straight in the eye. Every time I start on a new project that I think has any risk of failure, I do something that most of us find very uncomfortable. It is not comfortable for me either, but I have learned that doing it is one of the best predictors and guarantors of success I know. I have already mentioned it, but let me be more specific.

Before I ever take action, I ask myself these questions:

1. What is the worst thing that could happen if I try this?
2. Can I survive if the worst thing goes wrong?
3. If the worst happens, can I do more than just survive the failure? Can I rebuild my dream and try again?

When asking these questions, I mean can I survive economically, and can the relationships that I cherish survive. (I am not thinking about the kind of physical survival that could happen in a war or natural disaster.) My experience has been that in almost all cases, even the worst-case situations of economic loss can be overcome, but looking at the risks squarely in the beginning takes fear out of equation.

Fear of failure is often a primary cause of actual failure because of one basic reason. Fear of failure causes us to give less than our best. It is human nature to build in an excuse like, "I could have succeeded, but I didn't have the chance to give it my full attention." Whatever that excuse is, banish it from the beginning. It is a little scary to put all your hopes and dreams into a project, but anything less almost guarantees failure.

The saying, "Don't put all your eggs in one basket" doesn't apply in starting a business. Mark Twain turned this one into a saying that is much better when you are talking about committing to a project. He said something like, "Put all your eggs in one basket **and watch that basket.**"

The lesson from all this is very simple. Look the risk of failure squarely in the eye and decide if you can deal with that outcome if it happens. If you think you can handle it, commit completely. Then, make sure that the failure doesn't actually happen.

Every successful business I have ever created has had one or more 'near death experience' in which failure was possible or even probable. But because I had faced these possibilities in advance and was committed to success in spite of the risks, I managed in almost every case to turn potential failure into success. Out of eleven businesses I founded, only one failed. Even in that case, I saw it as the business that had failed. It was not my failure. I went on to experience more successes. You can too.

Let's look at an example.

In late 2007, I was co-founder of a biotech company that we had successfully taken public as a micro-cap public company. At that time, it had a public market value that was not large, about $150 million, but I had been able to recruit a superb CEO and had an underwriting commitment from an investment banking firm to raise $10 million dollars for the company. This would have lasted us quite a while, since our expenses were low. Also, we expected to announce some scientific breakthroughs that would have enabled us to raise a lot more money at a much higher valuation. The world looked wonderful.

Then, between November and the end of January, several very bad things happened:

1. The stock market began the decline, which ended in the crash of 2008 so our investment bank could not provide the promised $10 million, leaving us only a few months of cash before we would have been insolvent
2. The value of our stock crashed along with the market
3. My CEO unexpectedly died of a heart attack just *before* a scheduled insurance policy that would have saved the company was issued

Suddenly, I was facing some of the most difficult choices of my career.

Clearly, I had no hope of finding a new CEO to run a company that might be bankrupt in less than six months. That would be like finding someone to be Captain of the Titanic. It was clearly a no sale situation. My choices were either to take over as CEO myself and try to strengthen the company enough to attract a new CEO, or to shut the doors and deliver the bad news to our investors. The problem was that I had no experience as a CEO of a public company and no academic credentials in biochemistry. I definitely would not have hired me for the job.

The second problem was that the only way for me to keep the doors open long enough to look for a long-term solution was to raise a significant amount of capital from private investors in a very bad financial market. To do this, I would have to do two things. First, I would have to commit what was then a significant part of my own net worth to the company and second, I would have to persuade friends to invest with me, knowing we might lose all our money. I decided to commit my own capital. Then, I achieved the second goal by explaining my own commitment and letting each potential investor know that they might make a lot of money (which they ultimately did). However, if things did not go well, they would lose their entire investment, and if that happened, I would lose even more. In other words, I was not asking them to take a risk I was unwilling to take myself. Additionally, I refused to accept money from anyone I thought could not afford to take the risk, or from friends I might lose if things went badly. Reputation and friendships are far more important to me than money or saving any company.

The decision to put a lot of my own money into the pot raised significant fears of failure for me. First of all, the amount of money was not trivial. My net worth would take a major hit if I could not save the company. And, in spite of my efforts to be absolutely candid about the risks, there was the real possibility that I'd lose the friendship and trust of people I cared about. At that point, I did what I am recommending everyone who has a fear of failure do. I imagined the worst case that could happen and imagined what I could do if that occurred.

My conclusion was that, although it would hurt—a lot—I could survive the financial loss and that any friends who turned against me after I had done everything I could to warn them of the risks were not the kinds of friends I needed to preserve. I wrote my check, collected an equal amount from a small group of friends, and set out to save the company if I could.

The result, fortunately, was good. Over the next year or so, in spite of the recession going on around us, our stock price went from $0.15 per share to a high of $2.25 per share. Every one of the friends who had trusted me got an opportunity to sell at a very substantial profit. Over time, we also found outside financing and stabilized the company. None of this could have happened had I been paralyzed by fear. Either I would not have taken the risk at all, or I would have been consumed daily by my fears and would likely not have succeeded in turning the company around.

Ultimately, the company did suffer from the recession, and when I turned over management of the company to the investors who held the largest block of stock, the stock had declined from its high point. Still, it was worth far more than what the investors who had helped rescue the company had originally paid. None of this would have happened had I not taken steps *to directly face the very real fear of failure* that the situation presented, decide that the risk was something I could survive, and determine that the potential rewards were worth the risk.

One additional note is important in this story. At the time I made my decision to invest, I had many friends who were not investors with experience taking risks, who told me I was crazy. Had I listened to them or been concerned by perhaps having to be wrong and have them say, "I told you so," the company would have died. Fortunately, I ignored the risk of looking bad in the eyes of people who have nothing to win or lose because I understood their opinions were simply irrelevant. Yet, many people refuse to take action for just that reason – they don't want to risk looking bad to their friends. Looking at the real risks is important. But if we base our decisions on a fear of what other people may say, we have no business pretending to be entrepreneurs.

# CHAPTER 17

# Dealing with Failure

WE HAVE TALKED about the irrational fear of failure, but in the real world businesses do fail. That is just reality and is particularly true of startup businesses. Guess what? It is not the end of the world; it may just be the beginning of something better. I know that sounds like Pollyanna, but the truth is that, if handled properly, the failure of a startup business, particularly if it is your first, is both likely and not something you need to fear.

This doesn't mean you should not do everything in your power to plan for success and execute your business plan as perfectly as possible, but it does mean that you should not go into your first venture with so much fear of failure that you are paralyzed and cannot function at your very best. This is one place where the exercise I described in the previous chapter can be very helpful. Before you begin, try to imagine the worst thing that could happen if you failed. Could you survive it and go on? The chances are overwhelming that you can, with only a loss of some money that can be replaced and some embarrassment with your friends and investors.

So, let's talk about what failure is and how to deal with it. First of all, be sure it really is a failure and not just a message that you need to modify your business model, a process popularly known as a pivot. I talked in an earlier chapter about one of my early businesses where we first thought what we had was a new way of measuring the eye for LASIK surgery. It soon became obvious there was no demand for such a product, so we revised our strategy and tried to apply the technology to what we thought was going to be the next great thing, the early diagnosis of a childhood eye condition known as Amblyopia. Oops! That failed too. Both of our efforts embodied fatally flawed business models. At that point, common sense might well have told us to write off our losses caused by a failed technology and go on to something new.

Instead, we decided to try one more application of what we still thought was great optical technology. What we discovered was that the technology could be used to help surgeons doing cataract surgery to guarantee to their patients near perfect vision instead of a life wearing glasses. At one point the company was only a few months away from bankruptcy. Instead, a few years later, we sold it for over $300 million. This double pivot cost me and my other founders some portion of the profits we hoped to make because of the dilution (sales of new equity to raise more money, which reduced our percentage ownership of the company), but those who stayed with the company made a lot of money and had the joy of knowing that they had participated in changing many lives for the better.

On the other hand, I have been involved as an investor or Board member in more than one company that seemed to have a great future, but that we had to shut down and take our losses. Those losses were painful and embarrassing to explain to friends I had induced to invest alongside me, but because I have never recommended a company to friends that I didn't also invest in myself, I have never lost a friend because of an investment that did not work out. I have always made it a rule to be as honest as I can be when raising money, both to explain why I think the venture will succeed and to warn my investors that failure is always a possibility.

I also urge investors never to invest money they cannot afford to lose. Sometimes, I go one step further. If I think someone is investing beyond his or her risk threshold, I will refuse his or her money. This is tricky because if you talk a friend out of investing in something that becomes a huge home run, you risk their anger. Thus, I don't usually turn anyone down completely, but I do try hard to be sure the amount they are allowed to purchase will not harm their ability to live life as before. They may still be unhappy that they made less money, but if the deal is a failure, I know I have not severely altered someone's life.

From the perspective of the founder of the company, I know from hard personal experience that failure hurts, usually a lot. But I also know that I have never had a failure that did not teach me investment and life lessons that have helped to drive and inspire future successes.

Let me give you an example from painful personal experience. Rather early in my career as an investor/entrepreneur, a friend demonstrated to me a powdery substance that would instantly absorb huge quantities of water relative to its size. He also told me that the water thus absorbed would gradually be released as the substance reverted to its original solid form. My friend proposed to me that we form a company, acquire an inventory of the product, repackage it under our own brand name, and market it to farmers as a way of cutting the cost of excess water usage. We also learned that studies indicated that the gradual release of the captured water could increase crop yields by 10% or more and the product could last many years in the soil, repeating its water holding trick each time there was new rainfall or irrigation.

We had a product that no one else was offering to meet an obvious need in water-scarce California. What could possibly go wrong? Let me count the ways! We had made a variety of classic mistakes, but some of them were these:

1. We did not do adequate research to determine whether farmers would make the substantial capital investment necessary to buy the product.
2. The research data we relied upon was not sufficiently proven and available in scientific journals, so many farmers were not willing take a risk on what they thought might be a product that did no good and might harm their crops in some unknown way.
3. We failed to study the economics of our customers to realize that the very thin margins that farmers experienced in lean years made making a significant investment that would only pay off over multiple years simply not economical.
4. We failed to account for the fact that in California at the time, water used by farmers cost only a small fraction of what municipal users paid for water. In short, water was cheap and there was no incentive to make a long-term investment to save it.

These were expensive and fatal mistakes for the business, and each of them could have been avoided by: (a) not falling in love with how clever the technology was in capturing water and, (b) doing adequate research to understand what our customers needed and would pay for. "If you build it, they will come" is a clever line to promote a movie, but it is not a business strategy.

The biggest mistake we made, however, was that we saw all these problems fairly early on and could have closed down the operation before we and our investors lost a lot of money. Instead, we fell in love with our discovery and ignored what the market was telling us. It is sometimes incredibly hard to kill off a losing strategy or technology, but that toughness of mind is a key component of an entrepreneurial mind. Fortunately, I learned from these mistakes and have not repeated them, but I see all of them time after time in companies that come to me for funding.

In short, the potential to fail needs to be looked at coldly, avoided if at all possible, and learned from when necessary. As an investor, I can truthfully say that I have never refused to invest in a new project because the founder had tried something before that failed. My concern is not that it failed, but why, and do I think the founder has learned from that failure something that will likely make the next venture a success.

# CHAPTER 18

# Money

LET'S TALK ABOUT money. We can't talk about the tools of success without talking about it. Most everyone thinks they know what money is. And most everyone is wrong!

They say, "Money is the root of all evil." It's not. The quote actually says, "The **love of money** is the root of all evil," which is a very different thing.

In fact, until you do something with it, money has no value at all. You can't eat it; you can't drink it; you can't wear it (except perhaps as a silly costume); and it won't keep you warm—unless you set it on fire, but that won't keep you warm very long.

I recently visited the Federal Reserve in Los Angeles, where they have a room about the size of a football field completely filled with US currency. It is quite impressive and actually smells like money. But as long as the money sits in that room, it is totally useless.

But when you do something with money, it can become an incredibly powerful tool. And that is the way to think about it. **Money is a tool** -- no more, no less. It is a lot like those incredible Swiss Army Knives I grew up with that have blades for almost any task you can think of, whether cutting a steak or putting in a screw. It can be used for almost anything.

Once you begin to think about money as a tool, like a hammer or a screwdriver or a saw but incredibly more versatile, you have taken the first step toward being able to use money as a tool to change your life and the lives of those you love.

The really interesting thing about money is that it is a tool that can be made to grow to any size you need it to be to accomplish what you want to do. If you need something small like a hamburger, money can make that available to you. But if you need something bigger like a house or an education for yourself or your children, it can do that too. And if you want to build a huge business to try to cure cancer or create a new industry, it can do that too. The path to acquiring enough money to do whatever you need is different for a business than for a hamburger, of course, but the principle is the same. Money is a tool, and you can acquire that tool as you need it. And I really mean YOU! Not someone else, not some nameless corporation, and above all, not the government, but YOU, as someone who truly understands how the tool called money really works.

The bad news about this is that most people will never understand how to use the tool called money. They will spend their lives envying those who do, and buying lottery tickets, waiting for their luck to change. The good news is that if you are hearing or reading this, you are already on your way to becoming one of those people who understands how to use the tool called money to change your life.

It won't happen without work, but if you truly want to succeed and are willing to spend the time and effort to understand what money is and how to make it work for you—as a tool, not as your master or as a goal in itself—you are already on the first step of the ladder that leads to the top of the pyramid of success.

I frequently see examples of people who don't understand the true function of money when young entrepreneurs come to me seeking financing for their companies. Often, their budgets are woefully inadequate to bring the company to what I call the *success line*, where incoming cash exceeds expenses and can be expected to do so for as long as the company exists. The example of this that is closest to my heart is that of a dear friend of mine who is an author, host of a daily blog and a lecturer. The problem she had was that these were labors of love and she was literally working unrelated jobs to be able to support her passion for helping people through her blogs and seminars.

What we did was to examine what it would take to convert what she was giving away for free into a revenue stream without alienating the followers who needed her help. That led to the realization that the best way for her to reach the most people possible was to restructure her activities as a business instead of a non-profit charity. As a charity, she would have to spend an enormous amount of time fundraising. As a business, she would have the choice of funneling all of the profits back into the work she wanted to do and would actually have a chance to reach far more people.

Once we reached that conclusion, we built a budget for what kind of capital costs, start-up marketing, additional publishing, seminar costs (until they grew to become profit centers) and other start-up costs needed to be invested to reach her goal of impacting millions of lives. What became obvious when that work was done was that the new business needed to spend a modest amount of money in start-up costs, but could then become very profitable at a cost to the customer that was so reasonable that almost none of the people who had been receiving her advice and counseling for nothing through social media would be resistant to paying.

Knowing what the cost would be to get to her goal gave us a clear roadmap of what needed to be done and how much of the tool called money had to be raised. It turned out not to be a lot, but without using the tool of money as a way to build the business to profitability, nothing would have changed. She would have continued to think of money as just a way to pay expenses, never applying enough money to create a successful business. The difference is in recognizing that money is a tool, not just something you earn with a paycheck and spend to pay the bills.

Or, let's take an example that is public knowledge. Facebook is, by any standard, a very successful company, but there was a time when it was little more than an idea. Part of what made the difference between huge success and closing the doors on an interesting but unprofitable idea was the effective use of money. In the case of Facebook, a very large amount of start-up capital was required, but once that money was raised from venture capital investors, it was deployed to build the business. It became a tool to build market share, create a social media network, and solve the myriad of technical problems that growth creates.

But notice that the money was ultimately just a tool. For the founders, it was a way to pay the costs needed to start the business. For the investors, it was a tool to grow the business to something highly valuable. The key to that use of money as a tool was to start with an analysis of what needed to be done, how much capital would be needed to get there, and what the end result might look like if the venture were successful.

Once the founders and the investors agreed that the proper use of money to launch the company was likely to yield profits in the future, money flowed in, even though the company was not profitable for a long time. We'll talk in a later chapter about raising money for a venture, but the starting point is that money is not just something to be earned through your labor and spent to meet daily expenses. It is a tool to use in building true wealth.

# CHAPTER 19

# Money and Financial Freedom

LET'S TALK ABOUT a different aspect of money. You have no doubt heard it said that money can't buy happiness. This is true. I know many unhappy millionaires. But I know many more unhappy folks whose lack of enough money to feel safe in their daily lives creates its own unhappiness.

The truth is that having enough money cannot assure happiness, but it can assure freedom from many of the things that can turn even a happy life into an unhappy one. It is hard to be happy and joyful if you are not sure how you will pay the rent, or make the car payment, or take a trip to the doctor, or pay tuition for next semester. But the secret most people will not tell you is that having a good job is never enough. This is a dangerous belief to have—and yet it is all around us.

When I apply for a loan to refinance one of my pieces of real estate, the first thing I am asked to provide is a copy of my W-2 (the form you get each year to prove your salary and tax deductions), or a copy of my last two paychecks.

Since I have not worked for a paycheck for over 40 years, it always takes a while before I convince the borrower to look instead at the assets I have that provide enough income to pay all my loan payments many times over, whether I ever work a day or not.

What the people who write those loan applications don't realize is that a paycheck is the most vulnerable—and almost useless—asset you can have. The only asset that really matters is **the skill to make whatever money you need, no matter what.** Even having stocks and bonds and real estate is not as valuable as understanding how money works and how to create it in your life. You can lose the stocks and bonds and real estate through bad investing or a market collapse (although you never will when you really understand how to use money as a tool), but your skills will always be there as long as you have the health and strength to use them.

Don't misunderstand. It is important to build tangible wealth because someday all of us will be too old or too ill to use our skills, but without the skill of understanding how to use money as a tool for better living, none of your assets are safe. However, if you use the job you have to build skills that will survive the loss of that job, you are well on your way to the kind of financial security that means you will never have to fear losing a job again.

I have worked for two different very big companies that became insolvent and had to be sold for pennies on the dollar. With each of those events, my job disappeared almost overnight. Yet the collapse of those employers, and my job with it, had almost no impact on my life except to force me to look for new and better opportunities. Why? Because the skills I had gained could be translated into other jobs or, in my case, new businesses that created wealth and income without my having to work at all in those businesses. This left me free to pursue other dreams. And it all started with the fact that knowledge and skills, not a particular job, are what create financial freedom. Let me suggest a drill that I used when I was still employed by others to prepare myself to go out on my own.

Think of your current job, or a recent one you had, or the one you hope to get, and make a list of all the things you can think of that you could learn while doing that job that would make you more valuable, both to the current employer, and to other different kinds of employers. As an example, a counter clerk at McDonalds could study how the busy times corresponded to the employees on duty and thus learn something about staffing. Or he or she could study how McDonalds makes sure that everything it sells is prepared the same way so that a customer who comes in never gets something less than he or she expected, and that the experience is the same whether the store is in California or New York. Learning that would reveal one of the great secrets of successful franchising, replication of the consumer experience.

Using this *mental drill* in any job you may have is a form of on the job training that no school can teach, and practicing it can turn a boring job into something valuable and interesting. Let me tell you about a time I failed to follow my own advice. Actually, it was before I had learned the lesson of using any job as a learning experience. Many years ago when I was still a student, I got a job working for a government agency for the summer. It was boring beyond belief and largely consisted of sorting computer punch cards. If you are much younger than I, you will never have heard of those. We called them *IBM Cards* because they were made by IBM. They were conceptually similar to a primitive form of software and were used a way to sort and store data.

However, what they also were was part of the first baby steps being taken in those days toward what has become the modern computer. What I could have done, but didn't, was to study the theory behind the binary codes that are the basis of computer technology and perhaps learned valuable skills while getting paid for an otherwise boring job. But I didn't.

My life took a different turn, and by the time I graduated from Law School I was already illiterate in the language of computers. As a manager and founder of businesses, I have since taught myself (or been taught by patient experts who worked for me) enough about the digital world to evaluate what I am being told about the latest computer-based business that someone wants me to finance so that I am rarely fooled. But how much better would it have been if I had used that early opportunity to be at the front of the knowledge curve instead of at the back of the line?

Skills and knowledge are the crucial tools for building the kind of asset-based income that can give you true financial freedom. That is what I want to address next.

# CHAPTER 20

# Build Wealth, Not Just Income

EVERYWHERE YOU TURN today, you hear people lamenting the income gap between the top 10% of earners and the bottom 50% or lower.

These people are half right. There is a big difference between those who earn the most and those who just barely get by. But, the reality, there is *no income gap*. There are huge differences between what the richest and the poorest in our society have as income, but calling it a *gap* perpetuates a great myth that has been innocently spread by a host of well-meaning people in newspapers, TV and social media.

A gap implies a big empty space that is enormously difficult, if not impossible, to cross, a sort of Grand Canyon of income disparity. But there is a far better way to look at the differences in income across the wealthy, the poor, and everyone in between. Think of wealth differences as *levels on a pyramid* instead. If you consider a pyramid, there are lots of stones at the bottom, with fewer and fewer at each level as you climb toward the top, until finally, at the very top, there is only one stone or a very few brought together to form the cap of the pyramid.

But unlike the Grand Canyon, which no one could leap over, a pyramid can be climbed by anyone in good health who is willing to make the effort. It is not trivial effort, as I know from having climbed some of the great pyramids of Mexico (the authorities would not let me climb the pyramids in Egypt). As a result, most people look up to the top of the pyramid, but never attempt the climb. Others start out with great enthusiasm, but tire and stop halfway up. A few climb all the way to the top.

I submit to you that building wealth is like climbing a pyramid, not getting across a canyon with you on one side and the wealthy on the other. It is no accident that most people are near the bottom of that pyramid, or perhaps in the middle, but a long way from the top. It takes a lot more work, some luck to be sure, and some very clear goals and dreams to get to the top of the economic pyramid. But it can be done in part because there really are no gigantic gaps that can't be crossed. I mention this analogy now because there is so much talk in popular media today about how impossible it is to become wealthy today. That simply is not true. It is probably easier today than at any time in our history to work your way up from the bottom of the pyramid all the way to the top.

The reality is that anyone who learns the skills they need and develops the mindset of the wealthy and not the poor can climb the pyramid of success, create wealth, and never have to work again.

But first, let's remember what will **not** work—a better job or a raise will almost certainly not get you to the top. Think about it.

- In the US, to join the top 10%, you need income of about $250,000 per year. That is the equivalent of a salary of $125 an hour. The average family income for those who work for a salary is about 20% of that.
- There aren't many jobs that pay at least $125 an hour.
- And, any job you have can be gone tomorrow.

So what will work?

- There is a sign in Malibu, where I live, that says, "One good investment is worth a lifetime of toil." This is absolutely true. I have three investments in my portfolio that provide me all the income I ever need for daily living. Each of them was made years ago, and each of them now produces more income each year than the total of my original investment. I have other investments, of course, but those three always remind me of the truth of that sign in Malibu. No job could ever have done that.
- To create real financial security, what you need is to create wealth.
- A job is not wealth. A job is just income that can be gone tomorrow—although it can be a first step toward wealth.
- Wealth means that you have created investment assets that will work for you 24 hours a day. Wealth will provide for your retirement, help launch a career for your children, or fund a charity you love. If you build wealth, having a better job will never matter to you again.

But how do you start if you don't already have money?
- To create wealth, you need assets to invest.
- Cash is not the only asset. **Skills are also an asset** for all the reasons we discussed in earlier chapters.
- So forget about just getting a better job. A job--even a very good one—can be gone tomorrow. Instead, look on any job as an opportunity to learn skills and turn them into assets. A job is a tool—nothing more. It is a **tool** to help build **wealth and financial freedom**.

There are two basic ways to convert skills to assets:

1.  **Seek ownership opportunities**. Whenever possible, find jobs where some equity in the business is part of the pay package. Most of the new billionaires that you read about did not start the company that made them rich; they joined it when it was young and took part of their pay in equity. Steve Ballmer, who is a billionaire and recently bought a basketball team in Los Angeles, started out by going to work for a little start-up company founded by a friend of his. It was called Microsoft. In the beginning, there were some risks, but he undoubtedly knew that he had the skills to try again if the first company failed.

2.  **Use OPM**. This is just an abbreviation for *Other People's Money* and it is what you can attract if you develop skills that other people either do not have or do not have the time to use. I have a friend who just a few years ago suffered the complete collapse of the business he was in through no fault of his own. In less than five years, he has built a new business in a field he was never in before that provides him with a nice house, college tuition for his children, and expensive vacations for his family. The secret involved two things.

    *   He had developed skills that could be used anywhere.
    *   He knew he would need money for his new business and used the skills of language and persuasion to convince people with lesser or different skills, but who had money, to invest with him. He has made himself rich and his investors richer.

I built my wealth the same way and anyone with marketable skills can do it too—so develop those skills!

One more suggested drill. Take some quiet time to think about and write down *every way you can think of to trade your skills for the ownership of something that can produce value for you.* Let's explore some examples.

We've talked about broad-based tools like *belief systems* and *active imagining*, and we've talked about how to think about money and skills. Now, let's start getting more specific. No one would think of building a house without tools and materials, hammers, nails, lumber, and so forth. So what specific tools do you need for financial success? Over a lifetime, there may be many, but I have found that there are two that are essential. If you start with these two, all the rest can be mastered as needed. What are they?

### First: Master the English language and how to use it to persuade others to meet your needs!

Let me get personal for a moment. I have started ten successful companies in biotech, medical devices, finance, and other fields. Did I have skills in those fields? No! I never took a math course beyond high school algebra. I never studied science at all, and I didn't study accounting until my second year of law school.

What I did study was how to use language to persuade, excite and explain my dreams to others and to get them to support them. I found scientists who would develop the products, I found financial experts to fund my companies, and I found accountants and lawyers to guide us through the process.

If you truly understand the power of language—English in particular, and other languages if you can—you can learn anything else you need to know or find someone who already knows what you need in order to help you.

But if you don't know why "Me and him went to the store" is not acceptable grammar in the business world, or if you think the dialect of an ethnic group is cool and want to use it in today's business world, I can just about guarantee that you will fail. The reality is that in the United States and the other English speaking countries, English is the language of business and you need to master it and use it as the powerful tool that it is.

I realize that there are some who say that because Spanish is the native language of a large segment of the U.S. population, people for whom it is a native language should not be forced to use English. That argument may be aimed to please, and it is true that no one should be forced to speak fluent English, but the laws of success don't care about ethnic sensibilities. This does not mean that if your native language is not English and you speak with an accent or make occasional grammatical errors that you cannot succeed. One of the most successful businessmen I know has a very thick Lebanese accent, but it is obvious to anyone who works with him that he is making a great effort to use English and communicate clearly. Those efforts are respected and he succeeds, and a significant part of his business is public speaking. What he is obviously doing, however, is respecting the language of those with whom he does business. That respect earns him the right to make mistakes.

The reality is that people tend to do business with those who make them feel most comfortable, and speaking a common language is part of that. Also, if I am dealing with someone who has not demonstrated that they are trying to learn the language of the country where they are working, I am going to be wonder what other differences we have that might matter. Why risk alienating a potential customer or a source of financing by not doing your best to master the language of the country in which you live and work? If I decided to move to France and do business there, I would make it my very first priority to learn that language—and learn it quickly and well. You never want to make it any harder than necessary for people to do business with you, and that includes mastering basic communication skills.

This is just common sense, but it is astonishing how many people ignore it. Perhaps even more mysterious is someone whose native language is English and yet they don't take the time and trouble to speak English clearly or master the rules of grammar and spelling. The signal this sends to a potential customer or financing source is that you are not likely going to be easy to talk to. Difference is alienating, and what you really want is to develop the skills that will be needed to reach out to those potential partners, investors and customers so that you can tell them why they want what you have to offer and persuade them to work with you.

I have dealt with many highly successful black entrepreneurs and corporate executives. Some used a black dialect that they perhaps could never lose if they tried, but every one of them used the English language with skill and precision. I started my career with a distinct Southern accent. I have lost it now, mostly because of a conscious effort on my part when I spent some time as a radio broadcaster, but the accent never mattered. What did matter was that I never used the vernacular or made any of the many other mistakes that might have made others label me as poorly educated.

The upside of this is that, because true mastery of any language is not easy, and impressive public and private speaking skills are rare, if you make the effort to master them, you will find you have an enormous advantage. Along the way, get as much instruction and practice as you can in speaking and writing English. In business, you are always selling and before you can ever sell a product or service, you need to sell yourself. Language is a powerful tool. Use it!

### Second: Learn from those who are already successful.

You don't have to re-invent every skill. You can, instead, find someone who is already successful and learn from him or her just by observing, or, if you have the chance, by asking questions.

Tony Robbins, the motivational speaker who built his early fame by convincing people they could walk on a bed of coals, did not just build a fire one day and try walking on it. He found someone who actually did it, asked them how they did it, and then put that knowledge to work to begin building his fortune.

Notice some of the details of what he had to do to make that work for him.

- He identified the need to find a dramatic metaphor for success that would help him stand out in a crowded field.
- He found someone who actually knew how to walk on a bed of coals without injury, then arranged to learn from that person.
- He then used that skill to help make his programs a success and help build his own financial wealth.

My understanding is that he also did the same thing for the karate art of breaking boards or bricks with his bare hands and feet. He didn't spend years in a dojo learning martial arts. Instead, he found an expert to teach him what he needed to illustrate his message and learned just what he needed to know. That is being an efficient entrepreneur. In fact, when I saw Tony Robbins in a personal appearance years ago, he emphasized that he had made a point of learning just what he needed to know and sought out an expert to teach him the needed skills.

Warren Buffet, the most successful investor of all time, learned from his mentor, Ben Graham, how to find undervalued stocks; then improved on that technique and became one of the richest men in the world.

In my own career, I had a dream of starting a biotech company to cure diabetes, but I had no education in biology or any related field. What I did instead was to find the very best expert I could in the field, helped guide her in using her skills to create an outstanding scientific team and, finally, sat at her feet and had her teach me all that I needed to know in order to represent to the financial community what we were trying to do and how it could impact their lives and their wealth. With that, we created a successful public company and developed scientific methods that I believe will eventually help change the world.

There are hundreds of other skills and techniques you can learn, but it all starts with realizing that everything you learn, in school, on the job, or just living life, can be a tool to help you achieve success. Learning some of those skills can sometimes be hard work. But who cares? Once you realize that the skills are the tools to your success, the work can become pleasurable, because its purpose is to make your life better.

# Chapter 21

# Skills as Investment Assets

Consider these facts:

1.  No wealthy person I know depends on a paycheck to live the life they live. They own assets, stocks, real estate, and businesses that work for them while they sleep or play.
2.  A quality investment can last a lifetime, and beyond. A job is only as good as yesterday's paycheck.
3.  Most of the world's wealthy did not start out with a lot of investment assets. They first developed skills that had value and then converted those skills into assets. Every one of the young billionaires we see in the news every day got that way by trading his or her skills for ownership in a company they created or helped to create.

Let me share a personal example of how these factors can work. Early in my career, I developed some good skills in the area of finance. As a result, I got a job with a promising company in the real estate business. One day, I was offered a chance, along with other executives and junior executives of the company, to purchase an interest in a real estate project being developed by the company in conjunction with a major insurance company.

I didn't really have enough money to be able to make the investment comfortably—it involved foregoing some things I would have preferred to do with what little money I had—but I studied the investment until I understood it well. I was pretty sure I was right, and when I learned that the CEO and President of the company were also investing their own money, I decided to take the risk. For several years, I got nothing back on my money while the project was being completed.

Then something wonderful happened. One of the two apartment developments that made up about half of the total project was sold and my share was over 30 times what I had invested. The other half that was not sold has been providing me annual income for the last 35 years that is four times my original investment—each and every year!

You could say I was just lucky, but consider these things:

1.  I would never have had the opportunity if I had not developed skills that put me in position to be offered a share in the project.
2.  I was willing to use some of the very limited amount of money that I had to take a calculated risk on something that might move me up the economic pyramid. Notice that I did not take a Las Vegas type risk. I wasn't gambling. There was ample evidence from the actions of the more senior executives and my own research that this was probably a good investment. It was not a sure thing; nothing is; but the ratio of risk to reward was in my favor.
3.  I made the calculated analysis talked about in an earlier chapter and concluded that the worst that could happen was that I could lose that investment and that, although I wouldn't like it, I could survive economically if that happened.

4. What I didn't know then, but learned later, is that this
   kind of opportunity happens far more often than most
   people realize. I even made an investment a few years ago
   that returned over 100 times my original capital. It was
   not without risk, but I had developed over time the ability
   and confidence to think that, by using wisely the skills
   and capital I had, I had a much better chance of winning
   than losing and that the profits from my winners would
   far outweigh any loses on my mistakes. This is the
   formula for wealth.

Above all, it started with my developing skills that other people
wanted and needed, not just having a job. In fact, the skills that led to
that investment were developed through four different jobs that I held
until I had learned all that I thought I could from them. Then I moved
on and added more skills. Skills are assets and are worth more—and
are many times more secure—than any actual job you will ever have.

The art of trading skills for equity is one that I have found very few
people have. In fact, it is perhaps a key indicator of who has or is willing
to develop an entrepreneurial mindset. One of the sad things that I
have found in years of investing is that in far too many cases, employees,
particularly young people who are just beginning to enjoy some earning
power and the fun that comes with it, fail to take advantage of opportunities as they come along.

In more than one company I have started or invested in, we have
tried to do a good thing for employees by granting them stock options
or shares of stock. To my surprise, most of the people to whom we
offered such equity ownership placed no value in it and were instead
focused solely on how much cash they could get each payday. Since the

companies were usually in the early stages of their development with limited ability to pay large cash salaries, we lost those employees for whom cash now was more important than an investment in their future. They took other jobs with companies that paid more. In many cases that was a very poor choice and they watched friends who had stayed with us make millions of dollars.

But there is a risk in that and only those who have developed an entrepreneurial mindset will ever be comfortable with that risk. Some of the companies did not survive and those employees ended up working for lower wages and their stock options were worthless. But I suggest to you that, except for those who simply could not afford to trade any portion of their salary for equity, none of the people in the companies that failed wasted their time.

I have personally learned more from ventures that failed than from those that succeeded, for a very simple reason: when things do not turn out as expected, one can analyze the reasons and avoid those mistakes in the future. Companies that succeed sometimes do so in spite of major mistakes because they simply had the right product at the right time. That is wonderful good fortune, but when those employees or executives move on to their next project, the mistakes that were papered over by good fortune can sometimes prove disastrous in a different company.

This does not mean that each of us should not be thrilled when the equity positions we have taken are profitable. Success is wonderful. But even in the failures, there are usually lessons that can pay huge dividends later. In fact, although I have never seen an actual study of it, I strongly suspect that the vast majority of people who made fortunes in some emerging company have first experienced one or more failures. The United States, and some, but not all, other industrial countries have developed a wonderful perspective on entrepreneurial efforts. Failure of the company does not mean failure for the founders or employees. We are a people that give and cherish second chances and reward those who take risks in order to achieve success.

If you recall some of the stories I told of my earlier history, you may remember that two of the companies I went to work for failed and left me without a job. That was painful at the time, but those experiences made possible the success I later had. The reason was that I had developed skills that I could later covert into assets in my own companies and those I helped to launch.

**SKILLS ARE ASSETS. INVEST THEM WISELY,
AND WEALTH WILL FOLLOW.**

# CHAPTER 22

# Corporations as Wealth-building Tools

WE HEAR A lot of talk these days about corporate greed and many people, particularly young people, believe that their chances of success are being oppressed by the power and greed of big corporations.

Let me let you in on an important secret. There is no such thing as corporate greed. To understand why that is true requires that we realize that corporations are nothing more or less than tools, and the greed or altruism associated with them is no more or less than that of their owners or professional managers.

Thinking of corporations as some kind of enemy and failing to understand how they really work is a recipe for the failure of dreams. Think a bit about these ways to think about corporations.

1.  A corporation is a tool that enables someone with a dream to pursue it without fear that one mistake could destroy everything they have built or created for themselves or those they love. Suppose you made toys that children loved and were selling like crazy and both children and parents loved them. Then one day, through no fault of your own, a child injures itself with one of your toys and you are sued for millions. If the business were a corporation, that could still be very bad, but losing that

suit would not mean you lose your home or your car or your savings. Only the business would be at risk. A loss would be traumatic, but you could begin again. That is what corporations do. They separate the owners' personal assets from the risks of running a business.

2. That separation is what makes it possible for an entrepreneur to find the capital needed to start a new business. No one would have invested in Tesla Motors if they ran the risk that one defective automobile could wipe out their life savings. The same would be true of Uber, or Google or any other successful company. A corporation is what makes it possible for almost all the new innovations, from iPhones to electric cars, to happen. Without that thing called a *corporation*, no one would risk his or her money and nothing would ever get done.

3. But can't corporations be used for evil? Yes, of course they can, but in time, they will almost always be found out and go out of business. But that will not destroy the lives of the people who innocently believed they were investing in something good. The founders and managers of the corporation may have great difficulty ever getting money for their next venture and in some cases might go to jail, and the people who invested will lose their investment--- but not their most cherished personal assets. That is the magic of a corporation, and its power to do good as well.

4. A corporation is a tool, an incredibly useful one without which your chance of success would be much less. I use a separate corporation for each business I create or invest in and that enables me to enlist others to invest their money with me because we both know that failure will not

destroy us and we can recover to build a new great business.

Please allow me to get into the nuts and bolts of corporations for a few paragraphs. Not everyone reading this will know how corporations come into being and that is critical knowledge. The short version is that anyone can form a corporation. All it takes is the filing of some simple paperwork with the state in which you are doing business and the payment of some filing fees that are more annoying than burdensome.

Then, you need to keep records of meetings and decisions of your board of directors (even if the board has only one member—you), and there are annual returns for taxes and renewal of your license that have to be filed. That may sound a bit daunting, but, in fact, it is really quite simple and there are self-help companies like Legal Zoom or Nolo Press, and many others that will handle the paper work for you at a relatively modest cost. Just Google "forming a corporation" and you will find dozens.

My own recommendation, if you can afford it, is to spend the money to have an experienced lawyer prepare the papers and give you advice on which state is best in which to incorporate (it may not be your home state) and whether to use a standard form of corporation (called a "C" Corporation) or a Limited Liability Company (called an "LLC") or what is called an "S" Corporation. The LLC and S Corporation are specialized forms of corporation that allow you to take your start-up costs and operating losses as deductions on your personal taxes from other sources and avoid paying corporate taxes on distributions the corporation makes to you and other shareholders.

For the most part, tax considerations will determine the best format, but other factors may matter as well. For example, many investors, particularly professional Venture Funds, will only invest in C Corporations for reasons that have nothing to do with your business but have to do with their tax or business status. A lawyer who specializes in start-up companies will know these things and may save you a lot of money later.

Once you have created the legal entity you need, just use the *Dream Toolbox* tools you are developing and grow your corporation to whatever size you want and can. A corporation is just a tool, but it is an essential one for success as an entrepreneur.

# Chapter 23

# Greed, the Destroyer

Let me talk a bit about something closely related to viewing life as a zero sum game that we discussed earlier, but still different. With all that is exciting and optimistic about entrepreneurial ventures, a word of caution is in order. As you begin to be successful and have a few success stories in the bank, it is easy to become over-confident and, quite frankly, greedy. That impulse to greed can become what I call, *the great destroyer* because it can lead to decisions that violate all the precepts we have talked about in previous chapters. Let me give you a couple of personal examples.

Fairly early in my career, I had enjoyed some early successes in real estate development and was starting to look at equity opportunities in small companies. I was approached by a man who had been strongly recommended by an investor of mine for whom I had made quite a lot of money. His friend was in a business that I now know well and in which I subsequently made quite a lot of money, investing in what are called "micro cap" public companies. At the time, however, I was both ignorant of the field and eager to taste what seemed to me easy profits.

My friend's friend, whom I'll call Mr. X, described a small public company that he claimed not only had a potentially very profitable product (which it did), but was also subject to a lot of pressure from *short sellers*, or companies that sell stock of a public company they think is over-valued without actually owning the stock. (They borrow the stock they are selling then buy stock in the market to repay their debt after the stock has declined in price.) Short sellers serve a useful purpose in making sure there are always sellers as well as buyers for a stock. Some, however, with dubious practices will help "manufacture" false or dubious bad news so that they can buy the stock back cheaply. Mr. X claimed that *short sellers* had borrowed so much stock that they would soon be forced to buy back more shares than would be available to pay their loans meaning they would then be forced to pay almost any price to get shares, a situation call a *Short Squeeze*.

Based on Mr. X's story and my greed in hoping to make a huge quick profit, I bought a lot of stock without really doing my own homework on the world of short selling. As it turned out, Mr. X was in financial trouble because he had indeed bought a lot of shares that had gone down in value and desperately needed buyers. The problem was that the price stayed down, and then went even lower, so I lost far more money than I could afford to lose at the time.

There are several lessons in my sad story:

1. I relied on second hand information.
2. I invested beyond what I could afford to lose.
3. I invested in something I did not understand and had not adequately researched.

I survived my foolishness, but learned how easily greed can destroy wealth.

The second example did not happen to me, but I witnessed it. I mentioned it briefly in a previous chapter, but let me elaborate a bit more here. The essence of the story is that a very wealthy investor was bidding to buy a huge tract of real estate. Because there were only a few buyers who could afford such a large transaction, the wealthy man who intended to buy the property tried at the last minute to force the seller to take an even lower price, even though the price they had originally agreed upon was very favorable to the buyer. The seller just walked out, leaving the buyer wanting.

I was only a consultant in the transaction, but learned a very valuable lesson by watching the seller's attorney pick up all the papers and walk out of the room without responding to the new and unjustified offer. The proposed buyer tried to call him back, but he never returned, sold the property for his client to another buyer at the original price and the new buyer went on to become a billionaire from that purchase. The lesson was very basic and I have never forgotten it. When you try to take all the profit out of a transaction, leaving the other party with nothing, it will eventually lead to failure. As the saying goes, "In successful negotiations, always leave something on the table for the other party." If you don't, you hurt his pocketbook and his pride and are likely to lose both the transaction and a potential ally in the next deal.

Greed can be particularly pernicious when you are preserving gains that you may already have made through an investment, and I confess that I am still vulnerable to this type of greed and have to guard against it constantly. I'll give you an example. Not too long ago I invested in a promising privately owned biotech company at price of $2.70 per share. Less than three years later, it had become a public company and the stock had jumped up to $17 per share, more than six times my original investment and an annual rate of return of over 86% at a time when banks were paying about 1% interest on deposits. This was wonderful. However, I got greedy. Instead of analyzing the market and realizing that the value had gone up much too far and too fast to be sustained once the excitement of becoming a public company wore off, I sold very little of my stock and watched the price collapse from $17 per share to less than $8 per share. I lost over half my profit, a very expensive mistake.

A much smarter me would have realized that, although I thought the stock might ultimately reach $50 per share, it was almost guaranteed to experience some heavy selling first. That smarter me would have sold at least enough stock to recover my original investment. Then, if the stock declined and I wanted to own more shares, I would have had the money to buy them at a lower price. To be sure, I would not have made as much money had the stock continued to go straight up, and perhaps there are stock market techniques that I could have used to get a better result, but I knew I was not a stock market trading expert and let my own greed steal profits from me that were mine to harvest.

**_GREED IS THE GREAT DESTROYER._**
**_DON'T FALL FOR IT._**

# CHAPTER 24

# Buffet of Excuses

NOW LET ME turn to less pleasant stuff that is essential to becoming a successful entrepreneur, or even a successful human being in any job. There are people that I see every day around me—and you do too—for whom life is what a friend of mine calls a buffet of excuses. Whatever happens that is less than they hope for or is a disappointment of any kind is immediately assigned an excuse. *I didn't have enough time. My boss is mean. I had the wrong training. That's the way we have always done it.* And the list goes on like an endless buffet that guarantees to the person traveling down the line that there will always be another excuse so he never has to take full responsibility for anything. Everything that goes wrong is always the fault of some other person or event.

We've talked about this earlier in discussing blame and responsibility, but when I heard the wonderful phrase, *buffet of excuses*, I decided that some additional discussion would make sense. In any job, and particularly if you are working for yourself, there is an endless supply of opportunities to blame what happens on someone or something other than yourself.

The problem is that the process of blaming never results in anything different happening that might be wonderful, or even just an improvement. Dining at the buffet of excuses also guarantees that you may never savor the thrill of knowing that something wonderful happened and you were the one who made it happen. After all, if you are not responsible for anything that goes badly in your life and work, then how can you take credit, even in your own mind, for a great success? It is a boring way to go through life and it is deadly to the entrepreneurial spirit.

So how do we break that pattern and cancel the buffet? Let me suggest what may be for some people a radical idea, but it has great power. Instead of making an excuse for anything, suppose we took responsibility for everything that impacted our lives? Obviously, some things, like earthquakes or being run into while stopped at a traffic light are not within our control, but taking responsibility for how we react to such events—or how we did or did not prepare for them—changes how we deal with life itself. For example, could we have had a better earthquake preparedness kit available? Even if the conclusion is that we did everything right and the event still happened, there is still power in saying, "OK, bad stuff just happened. What can I do about it now that is within my control, not someone else's?"

The greatest power of leaving the *buffet of excuses* behind, however, is with respect to those things we can control, or at least influence. If your mindset is, *I am responsible for whatever happens today,* the subconscious mind will automatically start to look at what could be done differently or better to increase the chance of a favorable outcome. A backup plan will be made in case an employee or associate fails to do their job. If you were planning an outdoor party, you would not think of failing to have a backup plan if it rains. Why should there not be a backup plan if something goes wrong with marketing or sales in your business, or in the supply chain?

Some years ago, I was guilty of just the kind of thinking that I am now warning against. I had already made one mistake that no entrepreneur should ever make. I had agreed to share joint management responsibility with another executive in my company because he had a major financial investment. The result was that either of us could, in effect, veto the other. I still had a lot to learn in those days. However, that was just the prelude. The big problem was that we were launching a new retail product and I had devised a marketing plan that, if successful, would result in massive orders in the first 30 days. My co-executive believed that he was far more capable than I in handling supply chain matters. He no doubt was, but he also decided to delegate the actual implementation of supply chain management to a junior executive who had no experience.

The result was a disaster. We got the massive orders that we had hoped for, but could not fill them on time and had a very high rate of return because of packaging errors. Our distribution partner refused to do more business with us, I lost the confidence of a long time business affiliate, and the company almost went down, snatching an early major defeat from the arms of victory.

What could I have done? A lot! Had I listened to the inner voice that was saying, *What is our backup plan if supplies fail,* I would have had one and had at least a chance to avert the disaster. Instead, I had the choice of blaming my co-executive (which I did in part, but only inside my head) or taking responsibility and looking for solutions. I did the latter and we saved the business, albeit at a reduced level of sales.

What I had not done, and I hope I have learned that lesson forever, was to prepare the backup plan in advance. Instead, at some level, I was eating at the buffet table of excuses by saying to myself, "Well, if the supply chain is not adequate, it won't be my fault." What I should have been saying was, "If the supply chain fails, how can I prevent it from being a disaster?" Maybe I would not have been able to do anything anyway, but the very process of taking responsibility in advance would have made me a better executive and entrepreneur. Ultimately, if any of us wants to operate with a truly entrepreneurial mind, we have to take responsibility, not just for our own acts, but for those things we chose not to do. Only this has the chance of changing the outcome for the better. Otherwise, we are just looking for excuses after the fact and trying to find someone to blame. These are both useless exercises.

Harry Truman was right when he said,

**_"THE BUCK STOPS HERE."_**

# Chapter 25

# Don't Play the Blame Game

IN LIFE, LOTS of things go wrong for every one of us. What matters is not the event, but what we do with it. Suppose, for example, someone you trusted steals from you and causes you real harm. You have several choices:

You can **blame** the person who cheated you and always believe that, if not for that betrayal, you would have had wonderful success.

You can **blame** yourself and believe that, but for your foolish trust, you would have had wonderful success.

You can take *responsibility* for what happened, evaluate what damage control needs to be done, what steps need to be taken to prevent a similar event in the future, and then move forward.

The first two alternatives focus on *blame* and the harm that someone has caused. But *blame* creates weakness where what is needed is strength. It does so because *blame* implies a victim—in this case you.

*Responsibility,* however, is very different. It simply recognizes that everything has a cause and sometime that cause is something we did or didn't do. Sometimes it is just an external event like fire or flood. But even then, there may have been something we could have done or avoided doing that would have kept the fire or flood from harming us.

Taking *responsibility* doesn't mean you are a victim. It just means that you look at what happened and use it to make better decisions for the future. Could I have foreseen what happened and prevented it? If so, how can I avoid that mistake in the future and how can I solve the problems the mistake has caused?

Sometimes, you will realize that you made the very best decision you could have made with the available facts and that choice was just wrong. In that case, looking to blame yourself is not helpful. There is an old saying to the effect that once a cat has been burned by sitting on a hot stove, it will never sit on a stove again. But a wiser cat might instead just make the distinction between a hot stove that could burn it and a warm one that offers warmth and comfort.

If the decision was to trust someone who betrayed you, one choice would be to blame that person and avoid ever being vulnerable again by just doing the job yourself next time. A better choice would be to acknowledge that you were the one who made the choice to trust someone who betrayed your trust. Instead of never trusting again and trying to do everything on your own, the opportunity is to try to learn how to prevent a person you choose to trust from doing serious damage if you are wrong. Former President Reagan had a saying in negotiating treaties with potentially hostile governments, "Trust, but verify." All this really means is to give trust where needed to get a result, but to build in some protections in case the trust is misplaced.

The message in all this is that, except perhaps in a court of law, blame is a useless pursuit because it just makes you into a victim. *Responsibility*, however gives you power because it reaffirms that, ultimately, you and only you can decide what meaning to give to an event. You own it, so you can fix the problem, take steps to prevent it from recurring in the future, and learn from it how to recognize and avoid future different, but similar risks.

Let me give you a very personal example. Some time ago I was diagnosed with what is almost always a fatal and fast moving cancer. I was told that an immediate, but dangerous surgery might save my life, but would involve a long and difficult recovery. I was also told that some less drastic surgery might determine that the tumor was benign, but that by the time I learned if the diagnosis was right or wrong, it might be too late. Knowing that the chance that I had cancer was about 95%, I elected to have the more drastic surgery.

I was incredibly lucky. Mine was one of the 5% of similar tumors that was not cancerous. Great news! Except that I lost over a year of my life to recovery and will have some after effects for the rest of my life. I had two choices: 1) look back and bemoan the feeling in retrospect that I had made the wrong choice or 2) see if there were anything I could learn from the decision process I had used, and then just move on with life. I chose option two and am today happy and productive again instead of unhappy and probably not nearly as productive. *Responsibility* trumps blame every time.

Let me give you a personal example of how this can be applied in business. It doesn't paint me in a particularly good light since the problem I had to address was the result of some ill-considered decisions on my part. However, I think it will illustrate how problems can be approached as an entrepreneur instead of in a conventional manner.

Some time ago I decided to invest in some real estate projects being developed by a friend of mine. Then, quite suddenly, at least from my perspective, things took a very bad turn in my friend's business and it looked very much as if it would fail and I would lose my investment. Overnight, I went from anticipating a very nice profit to facing a major economic loss.

I had three choices:

1.  Walk away, take my losses and probably feel angry about it for a long time.

2. Engage in litigation that might have made me feel victorious, but would have been disastrous for my friend, destroyed our friendship, and likely still have caused me to lose all my money when he declared bankruptcy.
3. Accept that I had made a bad mistake and try to find a creative solution.

Although my friend's business mistakes had created the problem, the part of that problem that affected me was my own responsibility and I could either do something unproductive while blaming someone else for my problem (choices 1 and 2 above), or see what I could do to solve the problem.

Conventional wisdom would have said to follow strategy number two, hire a lawyer, sue for payment of my loans, and hope to recover some of the losses. I thought about that for a night, and then asked if there might not be a better way. Instead of initiating a hostile legal battle, I insisted on a face-to-face meeting to look at all of my friend's assets and liabilities and worked with him to find a solution.

It turned out that he had a significant number of valuable assets that were frozen because creditors had filed liens that prevented him from either selling or refinancing those assets. We determined what was needed to clear the logjam of creditors. With some financial help from me and from a new investor recruited by my friend, we were able to create a situation in which a plan of repayment was opened up, and everyone's needs were satisfied.

This solution avoided both anger and a loss and turned the situation into one that became profitable. I didn't do anything particularly brilliant. The solution, when looked at objectively, was obvious, but I could have destroyed the chance to find it by choosing blame instead of responsibility. That would have been a losing strategy. Don't do it.

There was no guarantee when I started those discussions that we would succeed—and I had been a darned fool to violate some of my own cardinal investing rules or I would not have had the problem in the first place—but by stepping back, not jumping into a legal thicket, and instead finding a way to look for new solutions, everyone became a winner. The moral, I suppose, is that, once again, every crisis has within it an opportunity. Finding that opportunity is how the entrepreneurial mind works.

# CHAPTER 26

# Luck and Preparation

I HAVE NOTICED that most people, when they meet or hear about someone who has been highly successful, think to themselves, "Wow, how lucky he (or she) must have been to be where they are."

The reality is that, although there is an element of luck in every success, there are many people who somehow manage to be 'lucky' a lot more than most of the rest of us. There is a reason for that and it is summed up in this frequently quoted statement: "Luck is where opportunity meets preparation."

Let's talk about good luck first. When we exclude such things as winning a lottery or inheriting a fortune from a long-lost relative, almost all luck is a matter of recognizing and acting on something that others do not see as an opportunity.

A dear friend recently told me the story of her parents. They were immigrants who lived in a Midwestern city, had worked hard all their lives, and lived a prosperous middle class life. But they had not reached financial freedom because they still needed to work every day to keep the revenue coming in. One day, my friend recalls, they commented over dinner on how cheap land was in the United States, where one could buy land around the city they lived in for $100 per acre. Although they were not rich, they could easily have bought quite a few acres of that land that would, in time, have made them wealthy and secured their children's futures.

Instead, they noticed it, but did nothing. In their case, the failure to act was primarily a function of the culture from which they came where such investments were not common because ownership of property was not protected well by the law—one of the great benefits of living in the United States. But how many native-born Americans read the same newspaper article, and also failed to take the action that would, today, have made them wealthy and financially secure? But they did nothing.

Why not? I submit to you that the reason was a function of two things:

1. Failing to prepare their minds to look around them on a daily basis for opportunities that others were simply not seeing or were ignoring.
2. A fear of taking a risk that might lead to a loss instead of a profit.

We have talked about the fear of failure and fear of risk, but let me give you another example of the difference between looking at the world with entrepreneurial eyes and failing to do so. I read recently about an entrepreneur who made his first fortune many years ago, when about 25% of the paper currency in the United States was backed by silver. Recognizing that silver was also used in industry and might in the future be worth more than the currency, he began buying paper currency that was convertible into silver and, when silver prices grew beyond the value of the currency, he converted the currency to silver. I am told he ended up making over $100 million dollars.

Why didn't everyone else do the same? It was printed right on the currency, "Silver payable to the bearer on demand." He saw this as an opportunity. Most of the rest of us just noticed it and did nothing. I was one of those who did nothing and had to make my fortune another way. Buy why? Like so many others, I had not yet developed the habit of looking at the everyday world around me as the candy store of opportunities I now know that it is. None of us will recognize all the opportunities, but failing to prepare our minds to see those opportunities is preparing to fail.

However, I later did notice that there was a lot of interest in using some things called *stem cells* as a potential way to treat diabetes. This time, I recognized the importance of what I was hearing and remembered that I knew a scientist who was one of the leading cell biologists in the world. It turned out she was looking for a new job or project at the time. We agreed to work together, along with another friend of mine who was brilliant at raising capital, and a few years later I was CEO of a public biotech company worth over $100 million dollars. Not all of that was mine. We had many investors, but it started because my partners and I saw something most everyone else was ignoring and took some risk to test our theory.

**It all starts with preparation of the mind to see opportunity where others see either nothing unusual or see problems instead of opportunities.**

# CHAPTER 27

# From Bad Luck to Success

WE HAVE TALKED about the fact that life presents all of us almost every day with opportunities for 'luck,' yet most people never realize the opportunities for good luck that they see every day. 'Bad luck,' however, seems easy to recognize. Bad things happen to us all, a flat tire, an auto accident, a loss in the stock market, a lost job, and hundreds of other things that all of us could name. We describe them as 'bad luck' and think there is nothing to be done except to endure it—or complain about it. I'd like to challenge that belief. With rare exceptions, almost all examples of bad luck can be changed into opportunity if we are able to view them differently.

Take, for example, the investors who lost half of their financial assets when the stock market collapsed in 2008. I know some of those people. For most, it was a disaster, but for some it became a great opportunity to acquire shares of wonderful companies like Apple, Netflix or Facebook at bargain prices. What was the difference between those who prospered and those who didn't?

The difference was preparation to succeed when times were bad as well as when they were good. Those who prospered during the recession of 2008 (and in the Great Depression of 1929 and the years after) had all prepared themselves for the opportunity by maintaining a reserve with which to purchase those stock market bargains. That preparation required an entrepreneurial mindset that said, "I know that this time of easy money and easy success will not last forever and I want to be able to benefit when things turn bad." This also meant not participating in the lust for profits so completely that they had no cash reserves when things turned bad. They did not stay away from the market completely, and that resulted in some losses, but they always retained financial capacity to respond to the opportunity that is at the heart of every crisis.

Let me be personal for a moment. I am one of the fortunate ones who had learned before the disaster of 2008 that if I wanted to be able to take advantage of opportunities when bad things happened, I needed to have capacity to act when there was an opportunity. I wasn't immune to what happened then. In fact, I lost about a third of my net worth between March and December that year. But I had retained reserves and the credit to take advantage of the bottom of the market, and ten years later my investments had almost tripled in value. This was not because I am a brilliant stock market investor. I'm not. My strongest skills are in finding and promoting promising start-up companies. But what I had done was preserve the capacity to keep doing what I did best, even when the stock market took away a large portion of my net worth.

But let me talk also about the ability of entrepreneurial mindset to convert personal tragedy into triumph. I know a woman who began to go blind from a disease that, so far, has no cure. She had small children and before she lost all of her sight, she quit her job and devoted herself to becoming self-sufficient and performing all the things that they would need, like cleaning, cooking, and just navigating around her home. Later, when her sight was gone, she told a close friend that her loss of sight had been a great blessing. Without it, she would, she said, have undoubtedly gone on working and missed the best years of her children's lives as they were growing up. It would be easy to dismiss this as just a rationalization, but I believe it is much more. I have no doubt that her life is as rich or richer than it would have been had she not lost her sight, not because the loss was not a tragedy, but because she was determined to find the opportunity that is hidden in almost all misfortune.

If we can apply that same kind of mindset to our financial and career decisions, there is almost nothing that can keep us from success.

One of the lessons I have learned from over 30 years of working with startup companies is that almost no success ever comes without what I call a *near death experience* of a financial kind. Some companies have had near death experiences that actually resulted in financial failure. Others have gone on to great success. What made the difference? Some part of it was luck, but we have already talked about the fact that the difference between good luck and bad luck is usually what response the 'lucky' person or company made to a given set of circumstances.

What I have observed in studying the successful people and companies I have known is that how the people involved dealt with the crisis that presented itself is usually what made all the difference. Flexibility of mind often revealed the most significant turning point. Let me give you a personal example, one mentioned earlier but which suits to illustrate this point well.

Some time ago, I started a biotech company that engaged in stem cell research. Because stem cells were controversial in those days, we could not find venture capitalists willing to provide the capital we needed. No one seemed to think it would be possible to raise money for a company that had no sales, and certainly no net income. But since without investors we would go out of business, we tried everything we could think of and finally found an underwriter who would raise the money we needed in the public markets. As one of my partners liked to say, "We kissed a lot of frogs before one turned into a prince." I think he was overly fond of fairy tales, but he was right. By knocking on enough doors and accepting a lot of *No's* without giving up, we found the money we needed and became a public company.

Our stock soon tripled in price and we thought we had found the secret of success. When we started to run low on money, we didn't think it was a problem because an investment banking firm (one that had turned us down the first time) now offered to raise $10 million dollars for us. That was a lot of money at the time for a company as small as ours, and we were thrilled. Then disaster hit. We were just weeks away from our closing when investment banks began to fail in what became the Recession of 2008. Our bankers said, "Sorry" and we realized we were only a few months away from bankruptcy.

However, I was confident anyway. We had recently hired a wonderful CEO with great charisma and a strong following in the biotech world. I was confident that he could find us the money we needed and I would help where I could.

Then, he died of a massive heart attack. Now what?

Those of us involved in the company still believed that stem cell research would result in cures for some terrible diseases, if we could only find the money to keep going. I put in as much of my own money as I could afford to show good faith and went on a money hunt. We called on everyone we knew, and raised enough money to last another six months.

But the drama was not over. We still needed more money and needed it soon. We kissed a lot more frogs and finally, through a referral from a key employee whom I would never have thought of as a source of financing, we were introduced to a foreign investor who agreed to meet me in Paris to discuss financing. I arrived in Paris only to discover we had a major communication problem because we had no common language. I needed a translator. This should have been easy, but it was the eve of a French holiday and no one was available at any of the usual translation services companies. Many hours later, with the aid of the Internet, I found a translator in England who knew someone in France who spoke all three languages involved, and we had our meeting.

We secured an investment of several million dollars, which enabled the company to survive until more normal sources of financing became available and the company survived. The lesson to be learned from this is not that failure is impossible, but that before declaring failure, the person who understands the *entrepreneurial mindset* will first look at the problem from as many different angles as possible and only if it is then clear that no solution exists will he or she abandon the project and move on.

By the way, I think it is important for anyone reading this who eventually raises money from investors to know that even in our darkest hours, we always told potential investors three things:

1. Our hopes and dreams for the company.
2. The reality that the money they invested might be lost.
3. If we succeeded, they had a chance to make a lot of money.

In the end, everyone who took the risk with me had the opportunity within a year to sell their investment shares for many times what they had paid, but I am convinced we would not have lost the trust of any of them had we failed. The reason: we were honest about our hopes and our fears and the risks involved.

That inspired both trust and hope, which enabled us to snatch victory from the jaws of defeat.

# CHAPTER 28

# Race, Gender, and Success

I NOW NEED to talk about a subject that evokes a lot of emotion for many people, race and gender. Yet, we cannot ignore it because how one views race and gender can make a profound difference in whether that person succeeds or fails in their economic life. I have a suggestion involving something as simple as the language we use that may make a big difference. I propose you change the word *privilege* to *advantage*. Let me explain.

We hear a lot these days about white privilege and gender bias. If you can change the way you think about these things, you can increase your chances of success in business and life dramatically. First of all, everyone who is not blind to reality knows that in the United States (and most of the Western world), it is extremely helpful to be a white male instead of black, Hispanic or Asian, or a female. I would be lying if I did not say that in the United States today it is a great advantage to be born white and male—and also an advantage to be born rich. But there is a huge difference between an advantage and a privilege.

In this, as in life, words matter. If you are black or a member of any other minority community, and I say to you, 'white privilege,' your mind may immediately think of some special entitlement that is granted to whites that you cannot hope to have. But if I change that phrase to 'white advantage,' notice how that helps you to see the world differently.

Let's take an example. If you are on a basketball team and are only 5'10" tall, and an opposing player is 6'10", he has an enormous advantage. But does it give him the 'privilege' of always winning? No. If, in your mind, instead of saying advantage you think 'privilege,' you will have missed a huge opportunity. Just having an advantage does not mean you win. That was proven dramatically in the basketball world a few years ago by a player named Muggsy Bogues. Muggsy was 5'3" tall, but became a star player in the NBA, playing against seven foot giants for 14 seasons in a league where even a 6 foot tall guard was considered too short.

His story is inspiring in its own right, but the point is that if he had considered being tall equal to the *privilege* of winning games, he would have stayed away, never tried, and never had the success he did. Other players had a huge *advantage* in their height, but advantages can be overcome. Did he have to work harder than everyone else? Yes. But he obviously considered his short height an obstacle to be overcome, not the lack of the *privilege* of being a basketball player.

I suggest that the same is true of gender bias. The reality is that life is not fair, it never has been and it never will be. But, particularly for those living in the United States, there is almost always a way to overcome any obstacle caused by race or gender. A black man was elected president of the US for two terms. A black man was for many years the CEO of American Express, a company that most people consider almost of symbol of white wealth. There are and have been female CEOs of several Fortune 500 companies. And with the passage of time, as more and more women and minorities succeed in high profile jobs and in politics, the *advantage* will be less.

A powerful example of success by a woman in spite of the obstacles of current society is that of Sheryl Sandberg, the Chief Operating Officer of Facebook and one of the richest and most influential women in the world. In her book, *Leaning In*, she talks at length about the obstacles that a woman faces in trying to succeed in a world that has been dominated by men for centuries. But the message is not about how hard it is to succeed, but about what a woman needs to do to succeed in spite of the disadvantage of being a woman. The reality is that there are real obstacles, but the other reality is that they can be overcome. Henry Ford's statement is still true, "Whether you think you can or you think you can't, you're right."

These stories and probably hundreds of others that research would reveal demonstrate that the key to success—whether you are female, a minority, or a white male—is to recognize that, while life is not fair, you dare not consider someone else's advantage to be a privilege; it is just an advantage that can be overcome. If you are part of a minority and see what others call privileges as just obstacles that can be overcome, you are very likely to succeed. On the other hand, if you are white and think that you are entitled to success as a 'privilege,' you will almost certainly fail and lose out to someone who worked harder and played the game of business and life better.

As someone who has founded ten successful companies, invested in many more and observed what happens in the real world of business, I am going to go a step further. If you are a minority, but take the trouble (and make the huge effort) to understand how the game is played, prepare yourself better and work harder, you can actually turn your minority status into an advantage. How can that be?

I am considering hiring or promoting two employees, one is a minority and the other a white male. They appear to have accomplished pretty much the same things, but both are young and have potentially long careers ahead of them. I am very likely, either consciously or unconsciously, to give preference to the minority person. Why? For the very simple reason that I care about who can add value to my company for the long term. If I am presented with two candidates who seem to have accomplished the same amount, but I know that one had to overcome larger obstacles to get where he or she is than the other, who do you think I am going to believe is more likely to succeed when my business faces the obstacles that every business does? I'm going to favor the one who has already proven that they can face tough odds and succeed anyway.

It doesn't always work that way. There is still prejudice in the world, but, particularly in business, hard work, skills that can be learned, and toughness of mind will usually prevail. So please, never think of 'privilege.' Think only of obstacles to be conquered.

To illustrate this in a different context, let me tell you the story of my friend, Karim. Karim at a very young age was a successful businessman in Beirut, Lebanon. At the time he lived there, it was considered the Paris of the Middle East by the many people who had visited there and by many who had never left their homeland. Then revolution hit Lebanon and Karim found himself captured by rebels who wanted ransom. After brutal torture, and with the help of a friend on the outside, he escaped with nothing more than the clothes on his back and the knowledge in his head. He ended up in Iran before its revolution and built a new and highly successful business. Then, once again, revolution destroyed all that he had and he narrowly escaped with his life.

This time, he ended up in the United States, again without any resources except his own determination and knowledge, and with the added burden of being in an ethnic minority. In spite of all that, Karim today is a successful businessman in a West coast city with a significant investment portfolio and a network of investors who trust both his skills and his integrity. This time, he is in a country where the risk of confiscation of his property is probably the lowest in the world, but what his experience demonstrates is that entrepreneurial skills and the refusal to accept defeat are the most important assets anyone can have to guarantee a life free of financial peril.

It would have been very easy for Karim to give up after the first or even the second disastrous setback. Instead, he is proof once again of Henry Ford's saying, "Whether you think you can or think you can't, you're right." The belief systems we build into ourselves matter, so make success a part of your belief system and nothing can stop you from achieving it.

# CHAPTER 29

# Victimization

I HEAR A lot of talk these days about people being victims of race, or their sex, or any number of other items. I'm convinced that this is one of the most pernicious perspectives anyone seeking financial success and security could have.

It is certainly true that under some circumstances one can be a genuine victim. You might be an innocent party in a car accident. You could be the victim of a drive-by shooting, or a natural catastrophe such as an earthquake or flood. However, I would like to submit to you that, even in these circumstances, if you're still alive when it is over, the question then becomes whether you continue to treat yourself as having been a victim and continue to dwell on what happened, or whether you look on yourself as someone who can overcome any kind of adversity. In the latter case, you will look back on the episode in which you were a victim as simply one of those things that happens in life, knowing that life is not fair, but that your job is to overcome the unfairness and create a life that you can both enjoy and be proud of.

When things get really bad, it worth remembering the statement of the famous German philosopher, Friedrich Nietzsche, "What does not kill me makes me stronger." Whatever your view of Nietzsche's philosophy, there is great wisdom in these words.

But there is another kind of victimhood that I find even more pernicious. That is the belief that somehow if you are a member of any kind of minority group, you are victimized by the majority. The most obvious permutation of this victimization is the belief that all minorities are somehow victimized by a cabal of white males. We have already talked about the fact that it is certainly an advantage in society to be a white male. There are advantages that you might not enjoy if you were a female or a minority race. However, as we discussed earlier, what you do about that situation matters far more than whether you have a distinct advantage starting out.

But something more destructive happens if you allow the attitude of being a victim to infect your thinking. It creates a built-in excuse for not taking action. After all, if you are a victim, what is the use of trying? However, I think the problem goes even deeper than that. Any of us who become accustomed to thinking of ourselves as victims forms an identity around that idea. Take away the belief of victimhood, and there is a void in our view of who we are. If we are not victims and that will no longer explain why we have not achieved our dreams, human nature immediately wants to replace that belief (it's really an excuse) with something else. It is very scary to think that we, ourselves, are the authors of our fates. How then can we explain our failures?

Those are very uncomfortable thoughts to have and they can be paralyzing in both our personal lives and in any effort we make to become successful entrepreneurs. Fortunately, there is a way to combat this *loop of failure thinking*. In Shakespeare's play, *The Tempest*, Act II i the character Antonio says, "What's past is prologue," suggesting that what's gone before is nothing compared to the great things to follow. I think this idea has profound meaning for anyone seeking to change his or her belief systems from *I can't* to *I can*. To me, this shift means that the past, including incidents of unequal treatment, are not defining moments that dictate our future, but are only a history from which we can learn. They should never dictate the course of our future. We can learn from the past, but if we let it dictate the future, we have lost the battle for success before we even start.

The mindset of victimization stops us cold. If we don't change it, every time we determine not to let some social or ethnic slight affect our future, our minds will simply substitute some new event of feeling victimized to fill the void we have created. It is scary to think that our lives and our destiny are completely within our control and that we alone are responsible for success or failure in our lives. But that is what every successful person does, one way or another. They take responsibility for the events that have shaped their lives, even if sometimes those events are debilitating and caused by others. What is never caused by anyone else, however, is how each of us responds to the events that make up our lives. Our response to the events that shape our lives has immense consequences.

If the events in our past—even if only five minutes ago—are negative, it is our choice as to how we deal with those events and whether we view them as instructive history or as defining moments. President Harry Truman is famous for saying, "The buck stops here," meaning that no matter who did something or what events had occurred, as President he had to take ultimate responsibility for what had happened and for what was to be done next. It may sound trite, but each of us is the President of our own lives. Other people or events may cause troubles to land in our laps or on our desk, but what we do about them is totally ours to decide.

By the way, the same is true of good things that happen. We may or may not have caused them. If caused by someone else, we must absolutely give credit to whoever did the good or caused it to happen. However, from that moment on, the buck stops with us. We can ignore the good fortune or build on it to create even greater success. We cannot control the past, but the future is ours.

This may all sound a bit philosophical, but the reality is that taking responsibility for the future and treating the past as a prologue from which we can learn, but which can never be allowed to dictate our future, is one of the key attitudes that separates those who succeed from those who do not.

# CHAPTER 30

# Appearances Matter

VERY EARLY IN my career I met a man who was trying to launch a new company. We were in Southern California, where dress codes were pretty casual, but at every business meeting, he was always dressed in a conservative suit and tie. I asked him why. He said, "I am asking people to take what they will see as great risks with their money. I need to appear to them as someone as solid and conservative as any banker." It worked. He raised the money he needed that time and many times thereafter, and he now is a very wealthy man. He was also a very fine businessman, but he correctly perceived that he might never have the chance to prove that if he didn't look the part.

That doesn't mean that a business suit is always the appropriate dress. But it does mean that when you are trying to persuade someone to do something you want, whether it is to give you a job or give you money for your company, you need to dress—and conduct yourself in speech and actions—in a way that affirms that you respect the values of the person you are asking to help you. If you are applying for a job as a disc jockey in a club, you would not wear a suit; but you would also not appear in a tank top and flip-flops. This stuff is just common sense, but it is hard to believe how often I have seen opportunities lost because the person who was doing the asking did not respect the culture of the person who had the power to say yes or no.

This can be particularly a problem for young people with minimal experience in the job market. Some time ago, I was interviewing young candidates for an entry-level job. Each of the candidates needed that job as a first step on the ladder of success. Several showed up for the interview wearing the baggy and low cut pants that were then trending in fashion, but that also carried associations with images of gang affiliation. The young men were not from gangs, but this was considered stylish in the crowd they ran with. I had no problem with this at a personal level and understood their reasons, but it created a problem for them in applying for a job.

In contrast, one young man showed up wearing a clean pair of blue jeans and a shirt with a collar. Guess who got the job? Was he the best worker or the smartest? I will never know for sure. He turned out very well, but I will never know about the others. They gave themselves no chance of being hired because of the wardrobe choices they made. On paper, the candidates appeared equally qualified, but the candidate who succeeded created his own advantage because he respected the culture of the business he was asking to join. My business dealt with the public and I knew that he would not embarrass or offend any of our customers. Once he passed my other tests, he was hired because he eliminated one additional worry that I otherwise would have had—how will he and my customers react to each other?

The same is true of adapting your speech to suit the audience and situation. When young people from ethnic minorities use vernacular language from the streets in interview situations, they are failing to recognize that the culture has a standard of acceptable speech. Refusing to recognize and honor the majority culture by speaking its language can be read as a clear mark of disrespect. The other reality is that the language of business, regardless of the skin color or ethnic background of the participants, is overwhelmingly mainstream English, not just in the United States, but in many cases in other countries as well. Not to learn and use the English spoken on Main Street and Wall Street signals a kind of disrespect, a lack of education, or a lack of situational awareness. None of these is good if your goal is to succeed in business or on most jobs.

Let me turn the analogy around. If I were trying to be accepted into a neighborhood street gang, I would do everything in my power to understand the language and culture of that gang. Using formal English and complex sentences would label me as both an outsider and someone who did not respect the culture of the group I was trying to join. It wouldn't make sense and might even be dangerous. So, why should someone who perhaps grew up in street culture think that they could demand of me as an employer or investor that I use their language? It doesn't make sense. Everything in life and business is about context, and the person who understands that and uses this knowledge, has an advantage from the very beginning.

I'll make an even stronger statement that is absolutely worth considering if you want good results for your efforts. If you are from an ethnic, racial or social minority and want to turn that into a huge advantage, then learn to speak the most perfect English you can, get rid of grammatical errors and slang, and speak even better English than the people you are trying to win over—whether as an employer, an investor or a customer—and you will likely have an advantage over the white man or woman you are competing against even when they are just as qualified as you are.

We live in a society in which it is beneficial for an employer to have as many qualified minority and women employees as highly placed as possible. Ironically, the result can be a form of reverse discrimination in favor of the well prepared minority person. Notice, however, that I said, "well prepared." If the candidate does not look, act and speak like someone who would fit into the culture of the business, then being a minority will hurt them. But if they have done their homework and use that knowledge, they will often have a significant advantage.

I wish it were not true that race, gender, and nationality matter. But they do, so if you are a minority, you might as well use that to your advantage, not by acting like a victim, but by speaking, looking and acting like a winner who understands the game of business. The game is not always fair, but it does reward hard work, good preparation, and a strong understanding of the culture of business.

By the way, the reverse of this is also true. We live in a highly diverse economy. If you grew up speaking only English and have willingness to learn and become fluent in another language, particularly one spoken by a lot of people in your community, you will have a huge advantage. Think about how valuable it would be to an employer dealing with the retail public to have an employee who was fluent in one or more languages beyond English. Or, think how valuable it would be to have a business in a multi-lingual area of whatever city you live in and be able to talk to your customers in their language. Context and respect for your customers is everything.

CHAPTER 31

# How to Start a Start-up Company

LET'S ASSUME THAT you have thought about all the things contained in the previous sections, have focused on a dream, done the necessary visualization, and are now ready to begin the day-to-day process. Let's assume also that you want to start a business instead of advancing your career within a company where you work. What are the first steps to take?

First, **define the need**. Whether you have just dreamed up a wonderful new gadget or Internet app, or you just know that you want to start a company and be your own boss, every successful enterprise starts with something that customers need. A friend of mine calls these *friction points*, which simply means that there is something all of us, or all the folks in some business, find frustrating or a significant impediment that needs a new solution.

As earlier described, some years ago, several of my friends and I were discussing new innovations in vision correction and realized that existing methods of measuring how the eye was receiving and processing images were just not good enough. We found an expert in optical measurement and another expert in laser technology and set about to see if there was a better way. We had two false starts because our market research said the use we had planned for our technology would have no buyers, but we finally came up with a plan that filled a genuine need.

Less than a decade later, that idea had grown into a company that we sold for well over $300 million. This is one way of capitalizing on a *friction point*. But there are other ways.

For example, I am often approached by entrepreneurs who want me to finance some new invention they have created. The first question I ask, before I even ask if the device works, is whether there is a need for what it does. If the would-be entrepreneur cannot convince me that he or she has done some market analysis and talked to potential users, and has reason to think there is a real market, I don't go any further. The most imaginative idea in the world is of no economic value unless someone (actually, a lot of someones) sees it as solution to some problem they have or an improvement to what they are already doing, so that they will buy it and use it when available.

There is a third kind of need that is far less often seen, but that can be enormously profitable. It is the need that no one realizes they even have, but once a solution is available, they can't imagine being without it. The original iPhone was that kind of idea. No one a decade or so ago that I know of had really thought about the possibility of using a portable phone to surf the internet, access social media, take photos, exchange instant messages, and listen to almost any song ever recorded and doing all this as you walked down the street. Yet, once Apple introduced the iPhone, which made all this possible, most of us can no longer imagine the world without it or the other brands of smart phones that followed.

These kinds of breakthroughs are less easy to identify than solving a problem that everyone knows about but no one has yet solved. But both are important to be aware of, and either kind of *friction point* can change the world and make the person who builds a company around that need wealthy indeed.

Note also that if you are working inside a company that has the ability to take advantage of such a *friction point*, you may have an opportunity to significantly enhance your standing, and perhaps your compensation and equity in your company. That is important because not every idea can be implemented by an individual entrepreneur, even with access to investor funding. The reason may be that the new innovation requires the infrastructure of the employer. Creating the iPhone, for example, would have been very difficult to do without the Apple platform to build upon. Also, it might have been impossible to do without infringing intellectual property of Apple.

However, I have seen and participated in several highly successful companies that were based upon technology developed by a large company but never pursued by that company for various economic or policy reasons. What happened was that an entrepreneur that learned of the technology, either as an employee or through some other means, was able to persuade the large company that had developed the original idea to license the technology involved, or give an option for a limited period of time to license the technology to the entrepreneur. With that license or option in hand, the entrepreneur was able to raise private or VC equity and develop the technology into a significant business.

My experience in this field has been with biotech and medical device companies and, as you know, I own interests in three such companies that have gone from a license to being public companies with market valuations in excess of $100 million or more each. That process provided free trading shares that gave investors freedom to sell and will give the founders access to future funding for their companies as their needs develop.

Although I have not been personally involved, the same opportunities exist in electronic technology and a variety of other industries. If you are working for a large company involving any kind of technology, it is well worthwhile to keep an open eye for these kinds of opportunities.

The next step is **identifying your customers**. This sounds a lot like defining the need, but it is a separate discipline. The trick here is to identify people who actually need or will want your product and determine how to reach them. I often hear entrepreneurs who come to me and say something like, "There are over 300 million people in the US alone and all we need is to convert 1% to our product and we'll all be rich." The problem with this is that it is a meaningless measure. It doesn't tell us who among those millions of people actually has a need for the particular product and how they can be separated into a group we can target for our marketing.

Identifying the specific group of potential buyers is critical.

There is no one way to do that, but every effective technique starts with an honest evaluation of what you believe the profile of a user of your product or service would look like. This is where market research can be critical, whether it is research from a fee for services firm or simply doing personal legwork and talking to as many people as you can who might be customers. What you are looking for is confirmation that you have, in fact, identified a category of customer that is both real and identifiable.

Once you have identified who your target customers are, a next step is to **estimate how many customers are within your marketing reach**. For example, if the only way to reach your target customers is a massive public media campaign, this may not be feasible without a major capital raise. However, in the early stages of a startup company, that is rarely the case. Internet marketing can also be expensive, but much less so. If this is where you think your customers are, you need to do some research on the cost of a website, including a shopping cart if you are going to sell online, search engine optimization, and other related costs. Find someone who has done this with a similar target audience and ask for help in estimating costs. You may be surprised at how helpful most other entrepreneurs are willing to be.

If your market is more local, simple tools like flyers and personal referrals may be all you need. The point is that failing to do this kind of research is simply failing to plan for success. Remember again John Wooden's statement, "Failure to prepare is preparing to fail." Don't do it!

Let me summarize and suggest that you use this list as a checklist to filter your own ideas as they occur to you. The list does not include everything you will need, but is enough to give you a point of beginning and a way of pre-testing your idea to see if it has the potential to succeed.

1. Does the idea you have address a genuine *friction point* that is either perceived by many but not yet solved, or is something that will cause people to say, "Aha, why didn't I think of that?"
2. Do you have access to the tools and technology to convert the idea to a product or service? If not yet, how could you get those tools through licensing, joint venturing with a person or company that has what you need, or by raising enough capital to develop the technology yourself?
3. What is your real market? Be specific about the demographics and specific description of your potential customer. Then determine how you can reach that customer once you are ready to start marketing and sales.
4. What do you estimate will be your costs of creating a market-ready product?

5. What is your specific marketing and sales strategy, and what will be the costs of marketing and sales until you reach profitability?

6. How much money do you need to raise or invest yourself in order to do all these things and reach profitability? (Then double that amount--all start-ups underestimate their costs.)

If you ask and answer these questions, you will have made a reasonable start. If the answer is that your great idea is just not marketable yet, don't discard it. Just put it on the shelf to mature, while you pursue another market that can succeed in the meantime.

Let me give you a personal example. Many years ago I was approached by a very smart entrepreneur with the idea of using some emerging technologies to grow meat in the laboratory. His idea was first to prove the technology in his laboratory, and then produce it for sale in a commercial facility, thus eliminating the need to raise and slaughter cattle. Since raising cattle for food is one of the least cost-effective food production channels in the modern world, it was an idea that had potentially great value. But, and this was a big "but," the technology was still in development and the end product did not look or taste much like a good beefsteak yet. Also, for most people at that time, the idea of eating "artificial" meat was not appealing at all. Neither the product nor the market was yet ready. The idea was put on the shelf and my friend went on to several other more profitable ventures.

He never returned to the idea, but today there are a number of companies, both large and small, working to bring artificial meat products to market. Times have changed and people are willing to consider such products in a way they would not have 10 years go. I suspect one or more of these companies will succeed. Sometimes an idea truly is before its time. If you conclude that this is true for your first idea, treat the process as part of your education and move on. You may or may not ever want to come back to it, but by doing the kind of analysis I have described, you will have saved a lot of potential grief and freed your time for something better.

CHAPTER 32

# Finding Money

THE REALITY OF any business is that it is very rare for it to succeed without first going through a period of losing money, or at least spending money for such things as equipment, inventory, marketing and people. Thus, there is usually a need to raise capital. There are several possibilities.

1.  **Use your own savings or personal loans**. This is the
    highest-risk way to proceed and should be considered
    only if you have reason to be highly confident that your
    product or service will sell quickly enough to reimburse
    your bank account before you run out of money. If you are
    one of those lucky few who can fund the early stages of
    your company long enough to demonstrate actual sales
    and a strong likelihood of success, you will not need to
    give up equity in your business or, if you eventually need
    capital for expansion, you will be able to get that capital at
    a much lower cost.

2.  **Borrow money**. Except by using your own credit, which
    is high risk, it is rare for a business to be able to borrow
    money on its own until it is well established and
    profitable. A possible exception is when you have

purchase orders from major companies that can be financed through companies specializing in Purchase Order Finance. I have invested in at least one company that is selling high profit-margin fashion items, using purchase order financing to cover the cost of manufacturing. Even then, however, the lenders will finance only a part of the price, so borrowing money and going in debt is usually not a viable choice for a new company.

3. **Equity Investment ("OPM" = Other People's Money).** I have learned that many people have negative feelings about the idea of using money from third party investors for several reasons.

   - Fear that they will get "ripped off" by investors and lose control of their company
   - Discomfort with what they consider "begging for money"

Both of these are groundless fears. The process and formats for raising investor money have been well developed and any good attorney who works with start-up companies can protect the founder of the company from unreasonable demands. Second, asking for investor money is not begging. The reason investors put money into a company are complex, but they usually include the hope of making a lot of money by buying a company when it is tiny that then becomes a major success. They also often include the fun of owning a start-up company that might become huge and give them bragging rights at the Country Club. Thus, if you present an investor with a true opportunity to do both of these things, you are doing them a favor, not the other way around.

We will talk about how you actually find investors and raise money in subsequent paragraphs and chapters, but for now, just know that it can be difficult and time-consuming, but is by no means impossible. You don't have to be rich to fund your dream.

For a new company, there are only a few basic places to look for money, so let's examine each of them.

1.  **Friends and Family.** This is a viable source of very early-stage money, but it has both advantages and risks.
    *   If things go wrong, you will have to deal with economic pain and hard feelings among those you love and who have trusted you. There is only one solution to this. It is not foolproof, but not doing it is foolish. Tell everyone from whom you accept money that they should never give you any amount of money that will damage your friendship if the business fails and they lose their money. Be clear. And if you know someone is taking more risk than they can really afford, don't take their money. The truth is that even this won't protect you completely. If you take less money than someone offers and the business is a huge success, they may be angry that you didn't let them invest more. And, if the business does not succeed, even if they only put in much less than they had planned, they still won't thank you for trying to protect them. Some will only remember that they lost money. It can be a good way to separate true friends from the fair weather variety, as challenging as that may be.
        In spite of these warnings, I know of a lot of companies that have used these investor sources very

successfully. In the Angel Investing world, we call these investments *FF&F money* (Friends, Fools and Family). However, there are times when it is the only money available and, if you succeed, (and isn't that the reason you started in the first place?) you will have very happy friends and family.

- One risk of using *FF&F money* is that it is very easy to over-value the company. That means, for example, that you might offer your family an investment that values the company at $5 million, only to find that when you go to the next round of more sophisticated investors, they only value the company at half of that. Then you have the problem of explaining to your family and friends why they paid twice what they should have for their interest in the company. The easiest way to avoid this is to provide that if the next round of financing is at lower price, the number of shares they will obtain will be adjusted so that they pay no more than the new investors. That will dilute your holdings as the founder, but is much better than the alternative hard feelings or worse, from your closest friends and family who have trusted you. The lawyers who prepare your investment documents can help you structure the paperwork for this.

2. **Angel Investors.** If you have the patience to go through the process, this is frequently the best source of start-up capital or the next round after you have used up your FF&F money. Thirty or forty years ago, when I first started founding and financing start-up companies, there were very few Angel Investors. Today there are thousands

throughout the country and around the world. The reasons are simple: 1) it is fun to be an Angel Investor because you get to look at all kinds of exciting new companies before they become successful, and 2) if you are good at it, you can make a lot of money. The downside for you as a founder is that you are usually dealing, not with one investor, but with a group of investors, each of whom has his own opinions about the structure or value of the investment.

Fortunately, most formal Angel groups, such as, for example the Tech Coast Angels in Los Angeles, have fairly formal processes for reviewing and pricing deals. The best way to locate which groups are active in your area is to start with the Angel Capital Association (https://www.angelcapitalassociation.org) and use that resource to find groups in your area. If you are fortunate enough to know someone in your area who is a member or has received funding from an Angel group, by all means try to get a referral from that person. Almost all Angel groups have a web presence and a procedure for online submissions, but there is no substitute for a personal recommendation from a trusted member or source.

The downside of using Angel financing is that the process can be time-consuming and the amount that any particular group can fund is usually limited, not by formal rules, but by logistics. For example, most Angel groups leave it up to the individual members to decide how much to invest in any one deal. The result is that you have to convince not one, but many potential investors to accept your proposal. All Angel groups have processes for handling this but it can often take 60-90 days, or more, to get from initial presentation to funding. Also, because individual investors usually like to make many smaller investments in many different companies rather than only a few large ones, the amount you can expect to raise is limited by the number of people who are in the group and the amount of group enthusiasm you can create. It is worth asking if you get past the initial screening process how long the path to funding usually takes and the range of typical funding sizes. That may mean that you need to engage with more than one group, and sometimes the groups themselves will help you do that. Don't be afraid to ask questions.

By the way, there are Angel investors who act independently and can sometimes fund an entire start-up round. The problem is that they are hard to find and will almost never accept a presentation without an introduction from someone they know and trust. The reason for this is simply that those of us who make such investments usually do not have a staff to screen investments. We often act alone. The last thing we need or want is a stream of solicitations from people we know nothing about. But if you can find such an investor through your network, they can be worth their weight in gold—almost literally.

3. **Venture Capital Funds.** Unless your company is in a field that is "hot" in investment circles, VC money is not likely to be a viable source for start-up financing. VC's generally like to put larger sums of money to work at higher

valuations than most start-ups can justify. However, if there are local VC firms in your area, it is worth trying to get an introduction to test the waters. I have found that it is often more productive to approach the VC you have in mind with a request for advice about their market rather than a funding request. Most—but not all—VC executives will be flattered by your request if it does not come with a request for money and will likely give you an up to date picture of who the players are in your area. You will, in the process of asking for general advice, have a chance to explain why you are asking. If the VC happens to be interested, you may be asked to present an investment summary, which is a significant toe in the door. If not, you have probably learned a lot and saved a lot of time. There is an old saying that is very true on this subject:

**IF YOU ASK FOR MONEY, YOU WILL PROBABLY GET ADVICE.
IF YOU ASK FOR ADVICE, YOU MAY GET MONEY.**

# CHAPTER 33

# Telling Your Story—
# The Investment Presentation Deck

WHEN THE TIMe finally comes that you have been invited to submit something to a potential investor, whether an Angel Group, a VC or perhaps just an independent investment 'Angel,' you will then need an *Investment Presentation Deck* to send or use in your presentation.

There are whole books devoted to preparing these presentations, and the criteria for what investors want changes constantly. For example, when I started in the business, everyone wanted a 30 page Business Plan. I haven't seen one of those in years. Times change. However, as this is being written, these are my recommendations.

1. Use Power Point or some similar presentation software that permits the blending of text with images. Once you have completed your deck, I recommend converting it to a pdf file format, as that usually produces a smaller file that is more readily downloadable to a smart phone. The best delivery method will change with technology, but you want something easily delivered and viewed that uses at least some basic visual imagery to catch the eye.

2. For in-person presentations, you should have a very limited number of slides, each with a minimum amount of text. One of the best explanations of effective

*Investment Presentation Deck* construction I have ever seen was that written years ago by Guy Kawasaki, the marketing man at Apple who put together the original campaign for the Mac computer. He developed what he called the *10-20-30 rule*. It's quite simple: a PowerPoint presentation should have **ten slides,** last no more than *twenty minutes*, and contain *no font smaller than thirty points*. Find more information on this by Googling "10-20-30 Rule."

The reason for using a simple structure is very basic. Any good presentation is designed to do more than present the facts, it must tell a story. Humans evolved as storytellers and our minds are wired that way, so if you really want to have someone buy into your dream, tell them the story of your Big Dream in as simple and exciting a way as possible.

If you are being asked to send a presentation in advance of a meeting, you may want to include more information. Even so, my favorite presentation is to have an initial group of ten or fewer slides that tell the story, then an appendix with whatever more technical slides are needed so that the reader can fill in the blanks that you would have explained in person.

3. Start with an introductory slide that tells as quickly and forcefully as possible why I, as an investor, should want to listen or read any further. I want to know:
    - What problem are you solving?
    - What are you proposing that is any different than what is already available?
    - How I am going to make a potful of money and get

out of the investment with that money and a substantial profit in my pocket in the next five years or so?

Other investors might have a slightly different list of what belongs on the first slide, but these are still the key questions for the opening.

Note that you need to be solving a real need or problem, not just improving on something that already exists. 'Incrementally better' seldom excites a new investor. And remember that how you present the 'problem' may matter a lot. For example, if I had proposed (before Apple), "I have invented a device that will improve the quality and reliability of portable audio playback systems," I doubt anyone would have been interested. However, if I were to say, "I have created a device that will enable anyone to carry thousands of songs in their pocket and play them at any time and add new songs without ever going into a store," that might have been pretty exciting before the first smart phone was created. Yet both descriptions are more or less accurate in describing the first iPod.

Remember, you are telling a story. Make it interesting from the very first sentence. Also remember that you don't have to be showy or dramatic to be interesting. In other words, don't get flamboyant like a presenter on *Shark Tank*. Just tell a story with an exciting beginning, middle, and end.

4. You will also need a very basic presentation of projected income and expense over 3-5 years and a statement about how and when an investor can get his or her money and

profit out (i.e. a sale of the company or an IPO) so that investor can calculate the chances of making 5-10 times her investment in five years or less.

Understand that we investors don't always get that kind of return or even necessarily expect it. I just sold an investment for three times my investment back in about two years and was delighted. If I could be sure of that kind of return, I would take that kind of deal anytime it was offered. Sadly, the reality is that a lot of deals that look really good, fail and result in a loss, so every investor needs to make up for the bad choices with the good ones. That means I need to see at least the possibility of a much larger return. My best return was about $160 for each $1, but I think most of us use ten times the investment as the measure of a "home run," so if the numbers and reality will support it, show me how that is possible. If the potential return is less, but you can convince your investor that the risk is also less, you may still be in very good shape, particularly if the investor thinks there is a chance that you could be wrong and the return will be much greater.

Behind the story you present, there also has to be substance. You need to be prepared to answer some core questions when asked. We'll get to those next, but they don't have to be part of the initial presentation. Your goal in an initial presentation is to create enough excitement that the potential investor will be asking you for more, so you don't find yourself begging him or her to look deeper.

In the course of a year, I will normally review many investment proposals covering a wide variety of business models, and some of those will progress to the point of my listening to a formal presentation. After doing this for years, I have come to realize the simple truth that *the most successful companies sell dreams, not products.* This is true in both the founder's financial presentations to me as an investor, and also in the marketing to customers.

What does that mean? Let's start with the customer part. Even if the product that is being sold is just a consumer product designed to simplify some aspect of daily life, the prospective purchaser is not so much interested in the specifications of the product as in what it can do for him or her as consumer. Perhaps calling that a dream is a bit excessive, but there is a lot of truth in the concept. If I buy a new Smart Phone, I don't care about all the technical wonders that are inside it, I care about what it is going to enable me to do that is either better than what I have now or is something completely different.

I recently bought a new Tesla automobile, paying about 40% more than it would have cost me to get a conventional luxury sedan with similar functions on the highway. I also realized with the rational part of my brain that my savings by using electricity instead of gasoline would never pay for the difference in price. Yet, somehow the idea of just plugging my car into an outlet in my garage each night and starting the next day with a 'full tank' of energy was so appealing that I bought the car. I like it a lot and it is an excellent vehicle, but what sold me was not any imagined savings in fuel cost or the various whiz bang features like automatic parking and hands free driving. I was sold by the vision (the story) of never having to go into a gas station again. That was the dream they sold to me.

I recently saw a presentation from a company that is selling a simple razor in a case that includes both a moisturizing spray and a skin softener that enables it to be used for touch up shaving by a woman on the go prior to a meeting or a social event. The company is successful, not because the engineer and packaging are excellent (which they are), but because they are selling to active women a solution to a problem that my female friends tell me is very real. That is the "dream" part. The buyer may like the packaging, but they are really buying what they think the product will do for them. They are imagining a situation in which it will offer a simple solution to a potentially embarrassing situation.

If you think about the products you use every day, there will almost always be that element of imagined benefit that the user sees. None of us buys hardware or services. We buy *solutions* to real or imagined problems or situations.

Most of my work is in the biotech and medical device fields, and the same is true there as well. Physicians may buy or recommend our device or drug, but the ultimate consumer is the patient. That person needs to imagine a positive result before they will consent to the use of the device or drug. A surgeon using the optical device I described in an earlier chapter does not say to his patient, "This laser will enable me to more precisely place the right kind of lens in your eye in place of the one I am removing when I cut into your eye." This would frighten almost all of us away. Instead, he says something like, "By using the latest technology available, I can assure you that when we are finished, you will see better now than you have ever seen before." This is a dream worth lying down on the operating table for.

Similarly, the oncologist does not describe the chemical characteristics of the new drug he or she plans to use. Instead, the message is, "There is a chance this will cure your cancer."

Now let's apply this same concept to the story that you as a budding entrepreneur might want to tell to me as a potential investor. It may be mildly interesting to me how cleverly you have put together the device or software you want me to finance, but what I am really interested in knowing are other things.

1. Is what you are proposing I finance going to solve a real need in the market place, or is it just an interesting piece of engineering or computer code?
2. How big is the market you are planning to sell to? Note that this doesn't mean, for example, how many people use computers or cell phones, but how many will need or want whatever improvement or new device or service you are offering.
3. What kind of profit can you make on each sale, and how much will it cost to produce each product?
4. What will it cost to market to each customer and will they be repeat buyers?
5. What do you believe will be your sales volume and net cash flow in each of at least the next three years?
6. **How do I get my money out, how soon, and how much profit can I expect to make?**

Notice that only the last of these items is ultimately important to me as an investor. All the others are just component parts of your effort to convince me that yours is a company I should invest it. The 'dream' you are selling me is that I will make money on my investment that is worth the risk. That is really what you are selling to me as an investor. All the rest is just supporting data.

Now, it may be true, as it is for me, that I am only interested in companies that I believe will in some way make the world a better place. Or it may be that I am only interested in some particular field such as the Internet, or biotech, or retail products, but those are supporting factors. If I am a professional investor, the 'dream' you have to sell to me is that I can make a lot of money. Otherwise, I might as well just give my money to a university that is doing research in the field that interests me or do something else that interests me. In this case, monetary gain (mine) is good (for you), but you have to sell me that dream of wealth or we will have both wasted your presentation time.

That is why I have so strongly urged every entrepreneur to learn the art of creating and using an *Investment Presentation Deck*. There are lots of books with more technical details about how to do this, when you're ready. Keep in mind that not preparing your presentation by studying how to make it great is just preparing to fail in your presentation.

# CHAPTER 34

# Support the Story with Numbers

ALTHOUGH YOU WILL only put summary financials in the presentation itself, it is critically important to have, as part of your back up information, a financial projection going out at least three years, and preferably five.

This need not be particularly detailed, but it needs to show revenue by source if you have more than one product line, the cost of goods that are being sold, and sales costs, so that you can come to a gross profit margin line. You will then also need a reasonable estimation of your general administrative overhead costs, so that you can calculate net income before taxes, or what is frequently called EBITDA. This simply means earnings before interest, taxes, depreciation, and amortization, and is roughly equivalent to pre-tax cash flow.

Investors will want to see that you have done the work to make those estimates, but the really important thing is that you build those numbers from actual estimates of your product sales by market segment. An example of what should *not* be done is what I see frequently, a projection which says, "The total market is X billion dollars and we only need to get a small percentage to be hugely profitable." This kind of analysis is a red flag for investors because it says that you have not really studied the source of your prospective sales. Also, the total market is only marginally relevant. What is important is the segment of the overall market that you are actually selling into. All of this requires some work on your part, but it will pay off when a prospective investor realizes that you have actually done ground up analysis rather than just plucking statistics out of the air.

You will also need an analysis of who your known competitors are. Any company that presents to me and says, "We really have no competitors" gets an immediate "F" and I seldom go forward beyond what politeness requires. Every business has competitors, and not analyzing who they are is a recipe for failure. They may not be making the product you propose or providing exactly the service you want to offer, but if there is anything like a real need, there will be companies trying to fill it. The most valuable companies are often those who fill that need in a new and more elegant manner.

To return to an earlier example, when the iPod was introduced, there was a significant market for portable disc players, but there were significant shortcomings like skipping and the relatively large size of the portable players. When the iPod came along, it changed the basis of the music distribution industry. Similarly, when home computer software was first introduced by Microsoft, there were other companies making computers, but operating them was beyond the skills of most potential users. That changed with the introduction of the Microsoft operating system.

Not every successful company has that kind of industry-changing potential, but unless something in the company can make a major difference that changes the user's experience, success can be elusive. Avoiding that problem comes from spending real time identifying who else is serving the same market you think should be yours and analyzing what those competitors are not able to do that you can. Showing that you have thought about your company's role in changing the consumer's perspective and habits of use can be a very powerful persuading factor in raising capital. More important, unless you do this work, you will not yourself know whether the idea you have is or is not likely to succeed.

There are a lot of other things to consider in building an investor presentation. One of the best ways I know to make sure you are not missing something is to go to the website of a respected Angel group like Tech Coast Angels and begin filling out their online application. If you can't fill in the blanks in that template, you probably have not done enough homework. If you can, that may not be all you need, but it is a good head start. Whether you submit the application or not is up to you, but preparing it is a very good exercise. See https://www. techcoastangels.com and look for a tab that leads you to the application for funding. Note that I am suggesting this website only because it provides a good template to use as a checklist. If you are in some other geographic area, find a group close to home. Most Angel investors will not go far outside of their own geographic area, so you will need to find a local Angel group to have any real chance of finding funding.

There are exceptions. I live and work in Los Angeles and recently bought shares in a Boston company, but that was because I was introduced by a trusted friend and believed their product (a potential cancer cure) was genuinely unique. In general, however, stay local. There is no reason to make a hard job harder by trying to convince someone thousands of miles away that they should bring their dollars to you. In fact, if you do go outside your geographic area, you should know that an early question that will be on everyone's mind is, "Why is he looking all the way out here? Couldn't he find anyone in his home city to believe in his company?" One way to find Angel groups in your own area is by looking at the website of the Angel Capital Association (https://www. angelcapitalassociation.org) for a group near you.

Once you have built your financial model, you will have a much better idea of what it might look like to an investor. By the way, no matter how carefully you prepare your financial estimates, *you will be wrong anyway*. No financial estimates of a start-up company that I have ever seen have turned out to be accurate. Some were too conservative, most too optimistic, but optimism is not a bad thing so long as you have done the homework to have a solid basis for your assumptions.

The important things about the numbers in your presentation are these:

1. That they support the story you are telling
2. That they give the investor an easy way to see what the company's profits will look like in the future so that he can calculate an estimated rate of return
3. That you are able to defend your methodology in presenting the numbers if you are questioned in detail, because you will have actually done the homework.

These back-up figures can all be put in a backup slide or even presented in a spreadsheet that is provided to the investor. Just keep in mind that before an investor actually writes a check, he or she is going to want to know that you didn't just make up your numbers from thin air. You may turn out to be wrong, but don't give away the future by not being prepared. Support the story with numbers.

# CHAPTER 35

# Choosing and Managing Your Team

MOST START-UP COMPANIES start either with a founder working on his own or with a couple of partners. Most of the really great successes in recent times have started with partnerships: Hewlett and Packard, Microsoft by Bill Gates and Paul Allen, Google by Larry Paige and Sergey Brin, and many others. There have also been highly successful individual founders like Jeff Bezos of Amazon, but they are rarer. However, whether you are on your own or have a founding partner, there are some key things that need to be kept in mind.

1. Whether you have an initial partner or not, it is important to have more than one person's brain working on the structure and formation of the new company. Thus, even if the project is solely 'your baby,' it is highly worthwhile to seek out at least one trusted and capable employee or Board member to act as your sounding board and associate in making all the early decisions that have to be made. Pick that person as carefully as you can, looking both at his or her skills, but also at how comfortable you are in working together and how willing you are to listen to ideas from that person, even if they are not what you want to hear. It can be very lonely and

isolating to be doing everything yourself and you will need someone to tell you when they think you are off track or offer new ideas you might have missed.

2. If you don't have a founding partner, provide some equity incentives for your first few employees that are sufficient to give them a sense of ownership in the company. But if they are employees and not true partners, don't give away so much that it will become a problem if you have to replace them later and have given away equity that you now don't have for their replacement. Except for a genuine partner, equity given to employees should vest over time so that if the employee quits before the job is done, most of the equity comes back to the company.

3. Document your agreement with your founding partner or first employees carefully, including what to do when one of you wants out or wants the other person out. The odds are high that at some point, one or the other partners will need to step into a subordinate role. A more mature company cannot be run like a partnership and someone has to be in charge. That often results in one of the founders or early key employees wanting to leave. There is no magic formula for how to deal with this, but spending a little money in the beginning on a good attorney with experience in start-ups to provide a solution may be money well spent to avoid nasty litigation or hurt feelings in the future.

Beyond the key one or two people who will be your real partners or employee 'partners' in the early stages, there are for every business some key gaps that have to be filled. For example, if your strength is product design, you may need someone really good at marketing and sales. Or you may be a sales genius but have no skills in manufacturing and production. Someone also needs to manage the financial and legal aspects of the business. These functions can often be outsourced in the beginning, but one of the initial founders needs to take responsibility to be sure that your company is getting the advice it needs to avoid problems and succeed.

Many decisions need to be made. For example, do you incorporate as a conventional corporation (known as a "C" corporation) or as a Limited Liability Company, which is still a corporation, but with different tax consequences? I have used both forms successfully. This is another case where getting some technical advice about your specific situation is highly beneficial. Even if it costs you a little in the beginning, it can save you a lot in the long run. What you do not want to do is operate as a partnership or an individual without incorporating. This creates too many legal risks in this age of easy litigation, and the advantages of incorporating in some form are just too great. Besides, it is almost impossible to raise capital without being a corporation.

As you expand your team after your initial funding, one of the things to pay attention to is whether the people you are hiring are motivated by cash or by the hope of future success. In the very beginning, you want, as much as possible, to hire people who share your dream and are willing to take a portion of their compensation in equity. This is important for two reasons:

1.  Those who share the dream are far more likely to be willing to put in the crazy hours that a start-up often demands and to deal with the problems that always occur on the pathway to success.

2. Cash will be tight in the beginning and everything you can save will be valuable.

However, as you grow, you will likely find that a significant number of people simply attribute no value to options or other equity compensation. These are the 'worker bees' and you still need them, but there is no point in wasting equity on them. It will not make them more loyal or willing to work harder because they simply don't understand the rewards of having an entrepreneurial mindset—or you can give them a copy of this book and try to convert them. Fortunately for you, not everyone has an entrepreneurial mindset or the field would get very crowded and no one would be able to build a business. We need the worker bees. We just have to recognize them for what they are and what they are not, as we try to recruit them to add value to our companies.

# CHAPTER 36

# Seeing Opportunity in the Ordinary

THE BEST ENTREPRENEURS see opportunity all around them in the things that most of us see, but do not observe. I was the fortunate beneficiary of something one of my partners noticed many years ago when alternative energy production was still in its infancy as a business. I would have missed it entirely, which is one of the benefits of having good partners and other smart people around you. Both of us knew that, not only could wind turbines produce electricity that the utilities were required by law to buy, but that the tax laws at the time made it almost impossible for an investor who was in the top tax bracket to lose money by buying a wind turbine. Lots of people saw that and there was a booming business in trying to create these 'tax shelter' investments.

What my partner saw, however, was that the patterns of wind direction and velocity were highly predictable in certain desert locations near urban areas in Southern California and that the government printed charts that showed average velocity and wind direction for almost all locations. Producing or buying wind turbines was expensive and difficult for small-scale entrepreneurs to finance, particularly since the banks in those days were not used to financing wind turbines. However, there was a way to profit, even without access to that kind of capital. It just required a different perspective to see the opportunity.

Although the turbines were expensive, both to buy and to maintain, land was relatively cheap in the areas near us that had the best wind patterns because people generally did not want to live and work where the wind often blew all day long and the temperature was often over 100 degrees. As a result, we were soon able to buy over 1000 acres of prime 'wind land' at a bargain price because the owners knew it was too sandy and too windy to be good farmland and far too windy for commercial enterprises. My share of that purchase has provided me enough income to live on comfortably for the last 30 years or more and shows no signs that it won't do so for the rest of my life and beyond. We did some other things that were more traditionally entrepreneurial to enhance the value of the land we purchased, but it all began with my partner noticing that land in the best wind zones was really cheap and we could profit by just changing the use of that land.

This kind of observation of ordinary things that others miss is intimately related to an entrepreneurial mindset, and is hugely valuable to develop. As you may recognize by now, I am talking about the ability to observe what I call the *friction points* in everyday life and ask what might be done about them. *Friction points* can be major problems like the lack of a cure for cancer, or such minor things as the lack of a way to walk and hear music at the same time, but let's focus here on some daily *friction points* because those offer the most readily harvested opportunities for most of us.

We talked earlier about the way in which the development of the iPod and then the smart phone changed the music industry. I remember well the inadequacies of Walkman and similar devices that depended on discs spinning in a box to generate music that you could carry with you. We all knew that existing devices produced a poor solution, but only when Apple came up with the iPod was there commercial success. Yes, it took a major company (although Apple wasn't that major then) to implement the solution, but the problem was out there for everyone to see and there were certainly other companies that could have built a device like the iPod. What was really required, however, was for someone to see that the existing way of doing something was as often annoying as it was helpful—then set out to do something about it.

I am sure everyone reading this can think of one or more other inventions that changed our daily lives that were really obvious once someone actually did something about it. What makes the entrepreneurial mind successful is that an entrepreneur not only notices the daily frictions in life, but also asks "what could I do about that?" and actually does something.

*What if?* is an enormously powerful question, but only if followed by action. And sometimes the right action only follows many failures. We all know the old story of Thomas Edison trying 1000 times before he got the first electric light bulb to work, but the lesson is still true. The problem was obvious, but it took someone willing to try and fail 1000 times to solve it. Fortunately, a solution is usually much easier to find, but it still requires a mindset that is willing to risk making mistakes and perhaps looking foolish in the process. But, oh, the joy of success is wonderful!

Let me give you one more example. Years ago, as I mentioned in the opening chapters, I was the chief legal officer for a company engaged in real estate lending. We had so much legal business in getting our loans closed that it became obvious we could save money by hiring our own lawyers and creating an in-house law firm.

Even though we created a lot of need for lawyers, our team still had time on its hands, so we decided to take on outside clients and handle their loan closings as well. At that time, one of us noticed that in real estate transactions, the brokers, as well as the title insurance firms, escrow companies and others involved often got most of their income only when the deal closed, and frequently got little or nothing when it didn't.

However, when the deals did close, the payments were often determined as a percentage of the total transaction cost. For example, if you sell your house, the brokers involved may get 5% or 6% of the sale price when the sale closes, but nothing if it does not. Yet, in the joy of a successful sale, few people worry that they paid a lot in brokerage fees. There are a lot of wealthy real estate brokers as a result. What we noticed was that lawyers never seemed to work that way, so we decided to try an experiment.

We quoted a fee that was a percentage of the transaction cost if the deal closed and nothing if it did not. We knew we could predict with a fairly high degree of certainty which transactions would close, and we had the safety of knowing that our parent company would pay our salaries anyway, so there was not a lot of risk.

What we learned was remarkable. My memory may be a little soft on the exact details, but what we learned was something like this:

1. In those days, a good lawyer earned about $150 per hour (try finding anyone at that rate today, but it was an earlier day).
2. When we divided our collected fees by the total number of hours worked on both the deals that closed and those that didn't, our effective billing rate was approximately $800 per hour, over 500% higher than standard rates for top lawyers, all because we took a carefully calculated risk.

The sad part is that after the parent company was sold and my law partners went out on their own, I never heard of any of them adopting the strategy we had already proven to be successful. Why not? I can only speculate, but my guess is that, even with all the data we had, it just seemed too risky. The entrepreneurial mindset just wasn't there. However, there was an exception. One of the lawyers observed something even better, which was that the real estate folk who were our clients made even more money. He became a successful real estate owner/developer and, when last I heard, had made many millions of dollars.

But, whatever the success story, most began by seeing the opportunity hidden inside the obvious *friction point*.

Let me share one more example that is still a work in progress as I am writing this. Everyone in the world of medicine has known for many years that time is the great enemy in treating stroke victims. If you can get the proper treatment to a victim quickly, his or her chances of recovery are far greater than if treatment is delayed, even if the delay is sometimes only measured in minutes.

But there is a further problem. There are two types of strokes. In the most common type, administering drugs that thin the blood causes the blood clot that in turn causes the stroke to dissolve more quickly can save lives. However, in the second type, the stroke is caused by excess bleeding in the brain. In these cases, giving a blood thinner can kill instead of curing the patient. This was the medical dilemma that everyone knew about, and no one had a solution for.

The founder of the company that was well on its way to creating a solution was not an MD or even a medical science PhD. He was an engineer with a specialty in nanotechnology. But in the course of the work he was doing on a different project at a major university, he realized that there might be a solution to the problem of emergency stroke treatment. He assembled a team, identified a potential solution that came out of the other research being done at the university, and used that vision of a potential solution to a major problem to arrange initial funding. As I write this, his company is on the verge of bringing to market a device that could save many lives and make the founders and those of us lucky enough to have been able to invest in this medical company a very handsome profit. There is still work to be done and obstacles to be overcome, but the future looks very bright.

But notice that it all started with an entrepreneur seeing something that everyone knew was a problem and asking the question, "Is there a solution to that *friction point*?" These opportunities are all around all of us constantly. For example, I knew about the problem with strokes long before I heard about the possible solution. I was just too busy with other things or didn't have the right kind of background to think about a workable solution. Someone else did, though, and that has made all the difference.

Fortunately, I have had my own share of *Aha moments* when I did see a solution others had missed. What interests me about this fact is that I do not have the kind of mind that sees solutions to *friction points* very often. Yet I have succeeded anyway. Why? The answer is that I have developed the ability to pay attention when others do see things that I have missed, and to help them find a way to turn those ideas into real world solutions. There is not just one route to entrepreneurial success. There are many, but unless you develop a lifetime habit of seeing opportunities in the ordinary and thinking about how it might become the next big thing, success is unlikely. This is a part of the entrepreneurial mind.

# CHAPTER 37

# Business Is Business—
# Leave Your Emotions at the Door

ONE OF THE earliest and most valuable lessons I learned as a businessman and entrepreneur is that it is very easy to allow personal emotions to cloud judgment and do permanent and unnecessary damage. In building businesses and transacting business, it is not uncommon for very acrimonious disputes to occur between co-founders, partners and friends. I have had the good fortune of having only four lawsuits over the 40 years or more that I have been in business. One every 10 years is probably not a bad record, particularly since I won three of the four for amounts totaling several million dollars and the fourth, the one I lost, was over a trivial amount of disputed money that I would happily have settled for, had the other party not sued instead of negotiating.

However, those four events, all of which occurred relatively early in my career, taught me a very valuable lesson, which was to never let a business dispute get personal. 'It's just business,' as they say. The temptation to be personally offended when a dispute is in full swing is enormous, particularly if litigation is involved. I can remember fantasies of the evil I wanted to do to a former partner with particular vividness. Instead, however, I kept all our personal interactions cordial and business-like. The result was that the disputes got resolved and I collected or paid without earning a lifelong enemy. In fact, one former partner, with whom I had particularly acrimonious litigation, later went out of his way more than once to give me information that saved or helped me earn many hundreds of thousands of dollars. We are friends today, all because neither of us fell victim to the temptation to turn a business dispute into a personal war.

This does not mean that you should be a doormat and let people step all over you. On the contrary, as word gets out that you will strongly defend what you think is right, but will not stoop to personal battles, you are far more likely to prevail. The reasons are simple:

1.  Everyone thinks more clearly when they put their personal emotions of anger and hurt aside.
2.  When you have a reputation of not engaging in disputes out of anger, but only when you have a reasonable belief that you are right, human nature is to take your position more seriously and believe that your claim probably has merit.

This attitude does not have to involve litigation. A couple of years ago, I went out of my way to advise a friend of mine on some business matters involving real estate, and even went so far as to arrange for him to be invited into a private investment group of which I was a part that was buying some apartment buildings. At the very last minute, he got cold feet—or bad advice—and backed out, leaving my partner, who had arranged the purchase, in a very awkward situation. We worked things out and found money (including some of my own) to replace the money my friend had promised. I then had a choice to make. I was angry that his change of mind had put me in a bad situation with my business partner, but elected not to let that anger infect what was otherwise a fine friendship.

The result is that we are still friends. I just won't invite him into any other business deals. And, as luck and good investing would have it, the extra money I put into the investment to cover the shortfall he caused returned 100% per year profit to me in the two years that we held the property. Sometimes the old saying, "Success is the best revenge" is correct. But my returns really had nothing to do with revenge or anger, and everything to do with not letting business infect friendships. That is one of the reasons, as I mentioned in an earlier chapter, that I am very careful about inviting friends into business deals without first having a candid conversation about risks, potential rewards, and separating business deals from our friendship.

There is a limit to this strategy, however. There is no excuse for anyone to commit fraud or lie about any critical fact in order to get an advantage, whether in business or life, and tolerating that kind of betrayal is never a good idea. Yet, even there, allowing personal emotions to affect our judgment or how we handle the situation is still a bad idea. Several years ago, the mother of a very good friend of mine was raped and murdered. Needless to say, it was a devastating emotional blow to my friend, but how she handled it reflected the highest level of wisdom and emotional maturity.

After an initial period of activity, the police investigation seemed to bog down as the officers involved were unable find the killer or link the evidence they had to their primary suspect. The case was apparently going cold. My friend could have stormed into the police station or gone on television demanding justice. Instead, she realized that this behavior might make her feel better for a moment, but it would not bring justice to her mother's killer. Instead, she very calmly but very firmly continued to press the police not to abandon the case, using whatever quiet pressure she could bring to bear, always keeping her emotions under control and her behavior calm.

The result was that, although the investigation seemed dormant, the officers involved never abandoned their efforts. A few years later, they got a break and today a killer is in jail. That would, I believe, never have happened if my friend had not pleaded her case with reason and determination instead of emotion and anger.

A woman I know quite well made a mid-life transition to a new profession from one in which she had been a great success, but which no longer suited her needs. She chose to pursue a new career in the real estate business. Early in that career, she found it frequently frustrating and anger-producing when brokers and sometimes colleagues, whom she should have been able to trust, would try to take advantage of her inexperience by tactics that were often highly unethical. Since we were close friends, I would listen patiently to the anger and frustration that she encountered every day. All I could do was remind her that it was 'just business' and so it could not be dealt with effectively through anger. Instead, she should counter it with professionalism and firm defenses.

Then, after a while, she had a realization and made a change. Instead of indulging in that anger or weakening her bargaining position by complaining to the management of the firm and appearing as a complainer instead of a winner, she quietly and firmly confronted each breach of trust directly, making it clear that she would not tolerate it. She also took firm steps to make it much more difficult for others to abuse what they had perceived as weakness arising from inexperience.

Very quickly, the word got around that she was not someone you could 'mess with' without paying a price. This didn't mean that she never had a problem with unscrupulous brokers again, but once she understood that quiet firmness was far more advantageous than outrage and anger, she continued to control of her life—and her professional emotions—throughout a very successful career.

**BUSINESS IS BUSINESS.**
**LEAVE YOUR EMOTIONS AT THE DOOR.**

# CHAPTER 38

# Delegate

THIS IS A short and simple lesson that is easy to talk about but often very hard to do. As you know, very early in my career, I worked as a young lawyer in a large and very successful law firm. One night when I was working late as young lawyers often did, I found I needed a simple document typed. It wasn't all that long and I was a good typist, so I went to my secretary's desk and began typing.

In the midst of my task, I sensed someone behind me and heard a booming voice say, "What do you think you are doing?" I explained and received the following reply, "We pay you for your time and charge our clients even more for it. The cost of bringing a secretary back to work, even if we paid triple overtime, would be less. If I ever find you doing secretarial work in this firm again, you are fired!"

The words were probably a bit harsh and over-dramatic, but I never forgot the lesson, which was that anytime you do a job that could be done as well or perhaps even better by someone else, you are wasting the most valuable thing you have, the time you will spend on this earth. Don't do it!

This lesson is essential to learn if you are ever to be truly successful in your business, whatever it may be, but it is not an easy lesson to put into practice. For one thing, when we finally get up the courage to try to start our own business and build our dream, we may think that no one else could ever understand our vision as well as we, so the temptation is to try to do everything ourselves except perhaps for the most mundane of jobs.

But the key to real success in building a business is something we in the venture capital world call *scalability*. In its simplest form, this simply means to remember to ask how your business can be made to grow from small to great. This always requires a team. No one person can ever do it all alone. The key to this is the difficult task of determining what parts of the work of the business can be effectively delegated, and to whom.

The first step in that process is simple, but difficult. You need to be brutally honest with yourself in answering these questions: What am I best at in this business, and what are my weakest skills (or what skills do I lack?) The answers to these questions can be maddeningly difficult. The temptation is to assume that the only things that can be delegated are routine tasks. But this is never true. You may be a terrific programmer, but if the company needs a great marketer of its product even more, and you are even better at that, then you have no choice but to find the best programmer you can and hire him or her. Then you can use your programming skills to monitor the work your new employee is doing and make a change if need be. But never take over all the jobs you *can* do by yourself. You have a more important job to do, and it is not programming!

Those are just examples. Your skills might make someone else the best choice for marketing. And, at some point in your growth, you will likely find that the greatest need is for someone to oversee all the various jobs that your success has created. Then comes a test that new entrepreneurs often fail. You may not be that person. I would guess that in four out of five, or perhaps more, successful companies, there comes a time when the founder, whose dream and 'baby' it is, has to step back and hire a professional CEO.

For many founders, that is an incredibly difficult decision. In my own companies, I always found it much easier because I adopted the attitude from the beginning that if I were still the CEO five years after the company was founded, I had probably failed. Only once have I had to violate that rule, and that was part of the history of a biotech company I founded and described in an earlier chapter. When a marvelous CEO that I had carefully recruited and hired to run the business died at the very beginning of a financial crisis that enveloped the entire country, I was forced to take control of a situation completely beyond my comfort zone. We were also running out of money and "Hello, how would you like to become the CEO of a financial version of the Titanic" was not a very compelling recruiting slogan.

In that particular case, I was forced by circumstances to keep the job of CEO, raise the money we needed by myself, and run the company until it was strong enough for me to recruit new leadership. My team and I succeeded, but I will never know how many other companies I might have launched in those five years, had I not been forced by circumstances to stay too long in a job that really belonged to someone else.

As you know, Mark Twain had a wonderful saying that went something like, "People say, don't put all your eggs in one basket." But I say, put all your eggs in the same basket—*and watch that basket!*" Successful delegating is somewhat similar, except that there are many baskets, each requiring special skills, and the company needs someone to *watch all the baskets closely*. The minute you are no longer the one best suited to that job, get out and find someone who is better. This is the ultimate delegation, yet you will still have your ownership in the company. The ultimate success at delegating is when you have launched a successful company, it is being run by people you have recruited, and it is making you rich while you start your next company or sit on the beach in Hawaii admiring the little umbrellas in your tropical drink. Such happy choices are only available if you learn to delegate.

### *DO IT WISELY, BUT DELEGATE, DELEGATE, DELEGATE.*

# CHAPTER 39

# Create a Monopoly

THERE IS A book that I think is very useful for every would-be entrepreneur to read. It is called *Zero to One* by Peter Thiel, one of the founders of PayPal and a prolific Silicon Valley investor. In it, he offers the proposition that from an investment perspective—and in many cases for society as well—monopolies are a valuable objective for any start-up to seek.

I won't try to replicate Peter Thiel's analysis. He has done it far better than I could possibly describe. However, I think it is worthwhile to talk briefly about the idea of creating a monopoly here. All the huge monopolies of history were at one time start-up companies. We have some very powerful current examples of companies that either are or are very close to being monopolies. Microsoft at one time dominated the operating system industry, and Google is in many ways a monopoly in its sphere, as perhaps are Facebook and Amazon, but each of these began by trying to create a different kind of monopoly.

Each founder started out by seeking to find a niche in their chosen market place that was either unoccupied or populated by relatively ineffective companies. Each also started with niches that were usually perceived as such small or uninteresting niches that there was very little competition. Facebook started as a way of connecting college students to each other, but few, if any, would have initially seen it as a worldwide connectivity system. Amazon began as an online bookseller when most of the world thought that was, at best, a small market that would never challenge the experience of browsing in a real bookstore.

In my world of biotech, the idea of harnessing the body's own immune system to treat cancer was for many years of interest only as an academic study area. Then a company called Kite Pharma demonstrated that it might really work as a cure for cancer and built a business that was sold for about 12 billion dollars. That was followed by other start-ups in the field, but as I write this, it appears that Kite and one or two others will continue to dominate this market. It all started as a niche market.

A company I know very well as a shareholder and director is Green Dot Corporation. It began with a niche market that no one was particularly interested in, the providing of pre-paid debit cards to teenagers. It is now valued at over $3 billion, dominates the industry of prepaid debit (which did not even exist as an industry when Green Dot was founded) and is fast becoming a leader in mobile banking (which also was not an industry when the company was founded).

I could go on and on identifying companies that became leaders in new industries because they realized before anyone else that there was room to dominate a niche in the marketplace in which no one else had shown much interest. They created mini-monopolies, then led the expansion of the niche until it became a major new industry.

Most niche market companies will never become a Facebook or an Amazon, but any would-be entrepreneur should look carefully at the fields in which he or she is interested and has expertise and ask whether there is an area in this world to become the dominant player, or in other words to become a monopoly. The niche may be a very small one, but as the examples I have given demonstrate, some niches that are tiny to begin with, can become huge. Even if the niche remains small, the company that can dominate it (have a monopoly in it) can often be highly profitable, providing its founder with an asset that can either provide income for life or be sold at a handsome profit.

The thing to remember is that profitable niches are easy to overlook. But the great advantage is that niche markets are usually a lot easier for an independent entrepreneur to find than for a big corporation that can only profitably look at opportunities that are obviously big enough to 'move the needle' financially.

Let me give you one final example that may be instructive. I have recently invested in a company from whose stock I expect to make a large profit. It began its life with a small group of scientists who had worked in large pharmaceutical companies and realized that there were promising drug candidates that were just sitting on the research lab shelves because it was too costly for the big drug companies to pursue FDA approval. The companies weren't trying to keep anything off the market. They just had too many other potential products in their inventory pipeline. Many of these drug candidates had become lost opportunities that were unlikely ever to be brought to market.

The scientists used their knowledge of the industry and their contacts within it to identify several drug candidates that looked promising, licensed the rights to use those products, and put together a plan to take the most promising ones to market. They made a good case for the potential value of the drugs they had licensed, some of which had been created by the drug companies spending many millions of dollars before abandoning their research. They then raised some capital from Angel Investors. With those funds, they did some highly focused research and animal trials and convinced an investment bank to fund the company. As I write this, that company will soon be a micro-cap public company with a market value that is likely to exceed $100 million in the near term and could be worth billions if any one of the four or five drug candidates they own is successful.

The point of this story is not whether I have made a good or bad investment, but that by finding an overlooked market that looked too small for the big companies to enter, a group of entrepreneurs have created a company that might both change the world of medicine for the better, and come to dominate a niche that is no longer small.

There is no formula for finding such niches that can become mini-monopolies, but being aware that they exist and actively looking for opportunities where others see nothing can be a formula for success.

**Then all your friends who now think you are crazy can say, "I knew him when…"**

# PART III

# SOME CONCLUDING THOUGHTS
# ABOUT THE ENTREPRENEURIAL MIND

# CHAPTER 40

# Choices Equal Freedom

IF YOU DIG a bit under the skin of almost any successful entrepreneur, you will find a core desire to have *freedom*. This does not mean freedom from tyranny or oppression, at least not in the United States or the rest of the free world. What *freedom* means to an entrepreneur is the ability to make his or her own decisions about what business to be in, what hours to work, what product to embrace, and a variety of other things. Beyond all of that, however, the successful entrepreneur simply has the freedom to live life as he or she wishes, without worry about what things cost or how to pay for the essentials of life.

This does not mean that to have freedom I need to have the ability to buy my own jet plane or have a mansion on the French Riviera. For me, such things would not represent freedom. But, I confess I know some for whom anything less would make them feel they were not truly free. Thus, economic freedom really means lots of different things to different people. However, I suggest to you that no one can be said to have real freedom if they know that their ability to pay their bills and care for those they love is dependent on whether they can go to work the next day.

That is why *building assets and skill-based freedom* are so important. I will never forget the sign that greeted me every day early in my career as I drove into Malibu, California, to look for investment properties. It said, "One good investment is worth a lifetime of toil."

This is largely true, but it leaves out an essential element of freedom I want to mention, which is that *no one asset—or even groups of assets— can ever leave a person free if he or she does not have the knowledge of how to use the tools* in their personal dream toolboxes in order to preserve that freedom. What really makes us free is to build an asset base that is diversified across many classes of business or real estate (or other asset class) and combine that with the entrepreneurial tools necessary to protect and enhance those assets.

No one can ever be 100% protected. Those who lost everything in the Holocaust, or in the Lebanese revolution, or in some natural disaster were definitely destroyed financially. But unless they also have lost the ability to use their minds and their experience to rebuild, these people still have the potential for real financial freedom because they know how to recreate assets in a world of chaos.

But let's return to talk of tangible assets. To create genuine financial freedom, the key is to own assets that will provide income, regardless of whether the owner can work. Although I work every day because I love what I do, I have also known for many years that work for me is completely optional and that, in the absence of war or some national financial disaster, my lifestyle is safe and I travel and invest as I see fit without worrying that I might not be able to afford a nice house and good food on the table.

I will take some credit for that. I worked hard and I saved a lot of my income during the years when I worked for others, but the other thing I did that *anyone else can also do* was to invest both my cash and my efforts into assets that had the promise of providing me future security. Sometimes I just made investments. Not all of those were profitable, but the winners outnumbered the losers and I never put all my assets at risk on one venture, so that no single losing investment could bring me down. The other thing I did was to trade skills wherever possible for equity in promising investments, whether real estate or companies. Some of those early investments that were made while I still worked for other people now provide a meaningful portion of my annual income.

My goal from a very early age was to reach a point in my economic life where, if circumstances ever prevented me from continuing to work, I could still live a comfortable life. I see around me far too many people who are my age, but never made the personal sacrifices of postponing new cars, boats or other 'toys' and will now have to work until the day they die to make ends meet. It is a tragedy of bad life planning that I hope no one reading this book will make.

By the way, I didn't have to forego 'toys' and other tangible rewards forever to get here; I put them off just long enough to build the basics into my investment strategy. I have had boats, second homes, and even for while an airplane, and have traveled the world for the last 40 years pretty much whenever I wanted. But I never did any of these things (except some travel—more on that later) until I had built an asset base to support me if my fortunes took a negative turn. It is not about specific assets; it is about mindset and the development of an *entrepreneurial mind*.

# CHAPTER 41

# Travel

LET ME MENTION one risk that I took long before I was anywhere close to having financial freedom, and that I recommend to every entrepreneur who wants not only to be rich, but to live a rich life. Many years ago, when I was out of work and trying to create a new career and my fiancé was changing her career, we discovered that we had a mutual love of travel, particularly what is now called 'adventure travel.' We were drawn to African photo safaris and trips into the jungle rainforests of Peru and Ecuador or the Galapagos Islands. We decided that, no matter what, we would take one such trip for at least two to four weeks each year.

We did this every year from then on, in spite of the fact that I was worried to death on several occasions that I would return to find some disaster had happened to my business while I was away. One foolish day, I remember being on a pay phone attached to a tree in an African game preserve trying to call my office in LA. Suddenly, I realized that no matter what that phone call revealed, there was not a darn thing I could do about it anyway and I was just ruining an otherwise magical vacation. I never did it again and now, in the digital age, I still limit myself to one checking of emails per day to ease my mind that no absolute emergencies have occurred. Even that much is probably silly.

Those trips did not make any direct economic sense, but they did something even more valuable. They guaranteed that my mind had a period of time in which to refresh itself and pushed me outside my 'comfort zone' of day-to-day thinking. I often returned with new ideas that were incredibly profitable and never in over 40 years did I lose any meaningful opportunity. Beyond that, my wife and I built experiences that will last a lifetime in memory and saw places and things that, in some cases, are now gone forever.

I particularly remember one couple that traveled with us for two weeks during our first African safari. They were a lovely retired couple who had waited their whole lives to travel to Africa. The problem was that by the time they had retired and booked their dream trip, the husband had developed severe arthritis and had to sit in our vehicle or in his tent at camp while the rest of us went out for hiking adventures in the wild. He still had many good times, but what a pity that he and his wife had not forced themselves to take that trip 30 years earlier! They would probably have found it so much fun that they would have taken many, many more over the years.

Years ago I heard the phrase "rocking chair planning," by which the person saying it meant to do the many things you want to do while you're young so that when you reach an age where life consists of sitting in a rocking chair on the porch of the retirement home, you will have a lifetime of memories. I don't plan ever to be sitting in a rocking chair on a porch for longer than an evening, but the concept is valid. Life is uncertain and memories are forever. Nothing makes better memories than travel. Give it a try.

CHAPTER 42

# Don't Fight the Problem, Solve It

IN MANAGING AND advising start-up companies over the years, I have observed an interesting pattern that often separates winners from losers. Every business—indeed every job, even if you are working for someone else—always involves a series of problems, some minor but time-consuming and annoying, and some that represent existential threats to the business.

The thing I have observed that makes a huge difference is a fairly subtle difference in mental attitude. Those who allow the problems to overpower them, seem always to view the problem as an opponent that must be attacked head-on and conquered. In business, where the problem is often financial, there is usually no head-on approach. If financing is not available when you need it, or credit is withdrawn at a critical time, there is no way to attack the problem directly. The investor or lender is only going to pull away more if you say things like, "But I desperately need the money," or "But you promised me the credit." These may both be true statements, but the approach is doomed to fail.

Some years ago, I had another kind of problem that would never have yielded to a head on attack. A supplier of a critical component of a product one of my portfolio companies was producing began shipping us defective products. They did not do so intentionally. Their manufacturing quality control and product testing was just not as good as they thought it was, and they didn't know how to fix it. Fighting the problem would have been to demand better products or threaten lawsuits if they didn't solve the problem.

In the meantime, however, we would have lost our customers and our reputation. Instead, we accepted that our supplier could not be part of the solution and looked for a solution elsewhere. The obvious one was, of course, to find another supplier, but the time lag to get the missing parts would still be too long. Instead, what we did was to be candid with our customers, offered to those who had received a defective product a full refund, and explained to those whose orders had not been shipped that we had a problem with a key component. We offered them a refund as well. That, of course, cost us money, but losing a customer who had already decided they wanted to try our product or continue using it would have been even worse, and would have threatened the survival of the business.

So, we went a step further. After offering apologies and a refund, we also offered an alternative. If the customer would allow us to ship later, the customer would get a free month's supply of the product. Note that the offer still cost us money, but we retained a lot of customers we would have otherwise lost, and since the cost of acquiring a new customer is often much more than the cost of the product itself (most businesses depend on repeat orders), we saved our most important assets, the customers themselves (at least a lot of them) and their good will and willingness to tell their friends that we had treated them fairly.

Here's another example. I mentioned earlier that at one point in my life I had borrowed a large amount of money, only to have the bank that loaned it to me demand payment on very short notice. My lawyers told me that I probably could have delayed the bank's collection efforts and kept the money for quite a while, but that kind of 'attack' on the problem would have failed in the long run. I was going to need continuing credit for this project and others, and being involved in litigation with a lender would have been a huge red flag in the face of those I might have approached for alternative financing. Also, no investors would have wanted to invest in a company facing legal action from a major lender.

Instead, what my partners and I did was to negotiate a short delay in the repayment demand. That was fairly easy because the bank did not want to end up only with a judgment against a creditor who could not pay them. They just needed to be able to show the bank regulators that they were taking steps to recall all their real estate loans, which was the reason they had called in my loan in the first place.

But I still needed to find the money. All the banks were experiencing similar pressures from the regulators to get rid of real estate loans. It was a really stupid policy because it disrupted a lot of fine business relationships needlessly when a more selective approach would have solved the credit crisis much better, but that is a story for a different book. What we did was to look at the structure of our business itself and create an investment opportunity that was very attractive to investors. That way, we raised money in the equity markets. Yes, that was more expensive than the bank debt would have been, but when the project succeeded, those investors made a nice profit, became loyal friends, and provided me equity for many other deals.

Part of what made that solution work was that, instead of *fighting* the problem and doing battle with the bank, which we might or might not have won, we looked for a solution that would enable the business to go forward. One of my partners, when faced with a choice of doing battle with an antagonistic party, used to say, "Is that the hill we want to die on?" In other words, is there a choice between fighting back directly against the people or circumstances that have created the problem, but perhaps losing the business or damaging it greatly, and finding a creative solution?

Of course, there are times when there is no alternative. But in the last 40 years, I have many times had the opportunity to bring lawsuits that I probably could have won, but I only did so twice, both when no other alternative was available. I won both of the lawsuits and received judgments totaling millions of dollars, but the reality is that I gained far more from the times I found a way to solve the problem, not fight it.

As I reflect on the thought process that has made this work for me, I think the answer is rather basic. Any problem can be thought of either as an obstacle or as a puzzle to be solved. Once we begin to think of problems as puzzles to be solved, not battles to be won or lost, we can begin almost to enjoy them—and definitely enjoy finding solutions a lot more.

# CHAPTER 43

# Stay Humble

HUMILITY IN BUSINESS is an often overlooked virtue and marker of success. This does not mean that you cannot be incredibly proud of your successes. But the truly humble entrepreneur/executive never forgets that his or her success is also the success of a lot of people who made it possible: the mentor who first showed you the potential within you, the investors who helped you get started, and the employees or partners who stayed with you when it looked as if the only light at the end of the tunnel was an oncoming train-wreck. If we truly acknowledge all those who have helped us along the way to success, it is hard not be humble. Yet we all know plenty of arrogant executives.

But humility does not mean failing to realize what you have built when you succeed, and sometimes you will need to stand strong against those who view the very fact of success as a lack of humility and will seek to bring you down. In Australia some years ago, there was a common attitude that I often see elsewhere as well. It was called the *Tall Poppy Syndrome*, which referred to the fact that in harvesting poppies, the ones that grow tallest are likely the first to be cut down. I don't actually know anything about growing poppies, so that may not be what actually happens, but the idea that if you don't raise your head above the crowd, no one will want to chop it off is very prevalent in business. This kind of false humility is debilitating to you and to your employees.

If, on the other hand, the founder constantly makes an effort to attribute successes to his or her entire team and avoids claiming all the credit personally, most of the problem goes away—and everyone working in the company gains a new sense of being appreciated. In short, with humility, everyone wins.

The other side of the coin is that when you find an executive who is always more concerned about job titles and the corner office, you have almost always found someone who either never had or has lost the thrill and satisfaction of entrepreneurial success. I had this demonstrated to me quite graphically many years ago when I was still practicing law. My client was a brilliant young executive who was building his business empire by buying and improving existing businesses that had lost their initial entrepreneurial momentum.

I was sent to negotiate the contracts for one of those acquisitions in a town thousands of miles from my client's home base. Because he was working on another acquisition that was larger, I was left, at a very young age, with the task of closing the purchase on my own. I had nightly coaching sessions with my client by phone and eventually got the deal done, solidifying forever my desire to be the entrepreneur, not the hired talent. In the process, however, I learned a valuable lesson about the difference between humility and arrogance.

A key executive in the company we were buying had long since ceased to be the powerful and effective executive he may once have been, but he was immensely proud of having a large desk, an important sounding title, and a company-paid membership in the local country club. As a result, he threatened to vote his shares to kill the deal if we did not guarantee those three things would continue. We did that, but also realized that we really needed to get him out of the company so that he would not be a constant troublemaker.

My mentor and client came up with a harsh, but effective, solution. We agreed to all three demands, but only so long as he came to work as a full time employee. Unfortunately for him, he overlooked one detail. When he reported for work the Monday after the closing, he still had his large desk—but it had been moved out of the corner office he once occupied and into the middle of the secretarial pool. Within a few days, he had quit the job and given up both his title and the paid membership in the country club. We would have happily kept his membership alive as part of the deal, but his arrogance in demanding a job title he no longer fulfilled and the corporate decorations that went with it became his undoing. A little humility would have paid large dividends.

I'm not particularly proud of the solution we employed—and in fairness, it was not my decision to make—but I have never forgotten the lesson that humility coupled with performance is far more valuable than arrogance and a title. I, for one, would much rather be sipping my tropical cocktail or starting a new business and cashing the checks from my investment than worrying about whether I was getting credit for being a business wizard. Stay humble, my friends. Those who really matter will always know what you contributed to the success of the business you created. Those who are not your friends won't matter.

# CHAPTER 44

# Gratitude Wins

LET ME TELL you about a business transaction I was involved in early in my career. I was in the investment banking business at the time, which meant my job and that of my boss was to find and arrange financing for our clients. One of those clients was a company in the real estate business, which had hired us to arrange a rather complex financing. We spent quite a lot of time working on that project and finally found a financing source. We were involved in final negotiations when something unexpected happened. A large corporation made an offer to our clients to purchase their company for a lot more money than the financing partners we had found were willing to pay. Our clients really had no choice but to accept the offer. They had investors for whom they had an obligation to get the best price possible.

Our company was just out of luck. In those days, fees were usually dependent on the deal being funded by the funding sources we found, so we got paid nothing if the transaction did not close. In short, "Nice try, but no payday." We licked our wounds and went on to the next project.

Then something happened that I will never forget. A messenger came to our office and delivered to my boss a check from our former clients for $100,000. In those days, that was a lot of money. (It still is, but was worth a lot more then.) Our client was just expressing his gratitude for both our effort and for the fact that we had accepted our defeat in the transaction without bitterness or complaints.

That simple act of gratitude remains in my memory today, almost half a century later. It represented two things that I think are an essential part of the entrepreneurial mind: 1) a simple gratitude for good fortune and the efforts of others that may have contributed to that good fortune, even if the contribution was not obvious, and 2) an expression of that gratitude without any expectation of reward. Our clients were superb entrepreneurs, as they demonstrated by going on to create great wealth for themselves and their investors. But they never forgot to be grateful for their success.

The result was that we did more business with them and they with us for a long time thereafter and I will always remember that simple act of gratitude.

This doesn't mean that all acts of gratitude have to be expressed in payments of money. Far from it. Often just a simple, 'Thank you' for a kindness offered or help given is all that is required. Sometimes there is not even a person or company to whom the gratitude is owed. It is enough that the person who is enjoying the success is grateful in their own heart for whatever people and events over a lifetime of activity have made success possible.

**I have tried in my career never to forget to be grateful and it has made my life richer by far. Try it. You'll like the happiness it brings.**

# Chapter 45

# Some Closing Thoughts

THANK YOU FOR staying with me on this brief journey through my experience of the joys and sorrows of being an entrepreneur. I hope I have succeeded in imparting a sense of how exciting and rewarding that journey can be without making it seem too easy or simplistic.

As I mentioned in the introduction, this began as a blogging adventure to try to open the eyes of young people to a world beyond just getting a diploma and reporting to work at a boring job for the next 40 years. As friends, and some strangers read the blogs on *DreamToolbox. com*, however, and shared their thoughts, I realized that I really needed to think about a larger audience.

I found that people of all ages were writing or calling to tell me how much they felt frustrated and unfulfilled, and often frightened, for their financial future, because they realized that the jobs and financial rewards they could see in that future were neither exciting nor secure.

I also realized that the problem was not a lack of written and audio material about the 'tricks of the trade' in creating an entrepreneurial business, but rather a failure of our educational system and our culture to cultivate *the mental attitudes and belief systems that could free almost anyone from financial fear, worry, and boredom.*

That is why I spend the first third of this book talking about the defining of big dreams and the creating of new belief systems and the tools needed to embed these systems so deeply into the unconscious mind that no barriers or setbacks could ever dislodge the core belief of *Yes, I can.*

I hope I have succeeded at least in part and for at least some who have read this little book. If you want to pursue some of the things discussed here more fully, I will be posting new ideas periodically at https://www.dreamtoolbox.com or Facebook at https://www.facebook.com/yourdreamtoolbox/ and other social media sites under the *Dream Toolbox* name. You can also contact me directly through the Dream Toolbox Facebook page.

I wish all of you well as you pursue your dreams, and, please always remember,

**WHETHER YOU THINK YOU CAN
OR YOU THINK YOU CAN'T, YOU'RE RIGHT.**

# AFTERWORD

## In a Nutshell, Here's Where to Begin

IF YOU HAVE made it this far in the book, you may well be saying, "That's all very interesting, but how to I use any of this in my life? My situation is so very different!"

Let me suggest to you that when you look beyond the external factors, including your current financial status, age, gender, race, and educational level—all the things that we tend to assume are critical to success for failure—the reality is that the most important thing you can do to change your financial reality is to **just begin.**

We all start from a different place in life, but I hope I have succeeded in convincing you that where you start is not what is important. You can just start where you are. What is important is what you do from this moment forward. There was a saying back in the '60s when I was young that said, *Today is the first day of the rest of your life.* It seems a little trite today, but is actually still true. For each of us, whether already financially secure or just starting out, even trying to dig out of a financial hole, the past is just the prologue. It is what you do next that is important.

So let me offer a few key summaries of what you have already read. These may make starting your financial journey a little easier and help you to take that first step, so keep reading!

1.  **Define Your Big Dream.** The early chapters of this book describe exercises like imagining what you would do if you knew you could not fail; then visualizing what life would be like to have achieved that dream as if it had already happened. These are without a doubt the most important parts of the whole book. I warn you that when you start, particularly when practicing visualization every day, you will feel foolish and may wonder, *What the heck am I doing this for?* But please trust me on this one. Just do it, and the changes that will occur over time will astonish you.

2.  **Begin Building an Entrepreneurial Mind.** The building blocks of an entrepreneurial mind are scattered throughout the chapters of the book, but perhaps I can remind you of some of the essentials that will give you a starting point and set of reminders to keep you on course.

    *   **Whether you think you can succeed or think you can't, you will be correct**. Develop an entrepreneurial mindset and make it stick.

    *   Banish from your mind **The Myth of *Someday*.** Today is the day to begin, not tomorrow or next week or next year.

3.  **There is always a solution.** Change your default mindset from seeing life's problems as barriers to your success and happiness, to seeing problems as simply puzzles to be solved.

4.  **Make a plan.** This is nothing more than taking your big dream into the reality of your day-to-day life. Sit down and create a step-by-step plan. *Failing to plan is planning to fail,* and this is absolutely true.

5.  **A job is not an asset, but it can be a tool.** Any job can disappear in a day, but the skills that can be learned in a job can create wealth that lasts for a lifetime and beyond. Bide your time, learn something every day, and save money for your future as best you can.

6.  **Life is not a Zero Sum Game.** And neither is business. Train your mind to look in each situation for ways to make the outcome profitable to everyone involved, whether emotionally, financially, socially, or in any one of many ways, and you will have mastered one of the key elements of financial success. Everybody wins.

7.  **Face the fear of failure and conquer it.** Before you tackle any project that creates fear for you, investigate what you really fear.

8.  **Money is a tool, not a goal.** Curing cancer can be a goal, creating the next Google can be a goal, owning a neighborhood business that lets you be your own boss can be a goal, creating financial freedom from worry is—and should be—a goal, but money itself is only a tool to achieve any or all of these goals.

9.  **Skills are investment assets.** We have talked about this at length, so I won't repeat it here except to say that in building wealth and financial freedom, *marketable skills are more important than any asset*.

10. **Race and gender will only stop you if you let them.** Make no mistake, being a woman or belonging to a minority can be a huge obstacle. But they are not brick walls, and society today is filled with people who have overcome those obstacles to achieve great success.

**11. Education is everything.** Education does *not necessarily* mean a college degree or graduation from a prestigious school. These things can help, but the real key is whether you have learned the basic entrepreneurial skills you need.

I hope you have enjoyed this book. More importantly, I hope you will use its content to change your life for the better and share the changes in your life with others. If you have found it useful, I hope you will share it with others. My goal has been to change lives for the better and every penny of profit from sales of this book will go back into the task of helping people change their lives for the better by achieving financial freedom.

There is one last thing I want to share. I have found that many people who want to start a new business struggle in taking the first simple steps to get things going. If you are one of those people, the following checklist may be helpful.

**First Steps to Funding your First Entrepreneurial Company**

1. Condense your business idea into what we in the industry call an 'Elevator Pitch.' This simply means that you need to describe in a few words:
   - The name of your company
   - What need your business is meeting or what problem it is solving
   - How this will make a difference to those who use your product or service
   - Exactly how your investor will make money
   The term 'Elevator Pitch' comes from the idea that if you were to meet a prospective investor getting on an

elevator, could you tell him enough about your business before the 30th floor to make him want to learn more. It is not easy. Work on it.

2. Create an *Investment Presentation Deck*. The days of 30-page business plans as fund raising tools are over. You still need to do the work like spread sheets, market analysis, income and expense analysis, but the Investment Presentation Deck is where that information is pulled together in a simple presentation.

3. Start the hunt for capital, using all the sources that are described in this book and elsewhere. And always remember, it only takes one Yes to launch you on your way.

**HAPPY HUNTING.**

Praise for
# www.DreamToolbox.com

"On it's face, the website, **www.DreamToolbox.com,** is a public service for young people who want to learn all about entrepreneurship directly through the life and learnings of Ken Aldrich, a successful serial entrepreneur who has done it all over a 50-year run. But as the videos play, the viewer soon develops a deeper understanding that **DreamToolbox** is more than a *How To*. Rather, it's an act of love and respect for young people all across America who, if not for **DreamToolbox,** would have never had the chance to meet a real life entrepreneur; let alone understand the life options for freedom, independence and control of one's own life that entrepreneurship can provide. Mr. Aldrich proves the old adage that *People don't care what you know until they know that you care.* The young people from all backgrounds and circumstances who watch **DreamToolbox** will know, without question, that Ken Aldrich cares and so they will clearly care about what he knows. **DreamToolbox** is a must watch for anyone seeking a better life through entrepreneurship; and, because of Ken Aldrich, viewers will now have a toolbox to achieve the best of America—the ability to become what you dream."

**—Steve Streit, Founder & CEO of Green Dot Corporation**